INDIAN COOKERY

INDIAN COOKERY

Grange
BOOKS

Published by Grange Books
An imprint of Books & Toys Limited
The Grange
Grange Yard
London SE1 3AG
By arrangement with Ebury Press

ISBN 1 85627 112 9

Consultant editor: Jeni Wright
Editors: Veronica Sperling and Barbara Croxford
Design: Mike Leaman
Illustrations: John Woodcock and Kate Simunek
Photography: David Johnson
Cookery: Susanna Tee, Maxine Clark, Janet Smith

Filmset by Advanced Filmsetters (Glasgow) Ltd

Printed and bound in Italy by
New Interlitho, S.p.a., Milan

CONTENTS

COOKERY NOTES

Follow either metric or imperial measures for the recipes in this book as they are not inter-changeable. Sets of spoon measures are available in both metric and imperial size to give accurate measurement of small quantities. All spoon measures are level unless otherwise stated. When measuring milk we have used the exact conversion of 568 ml (1 pint).
* Size 4 eggs should be used except when otherwise stated.
† Granulated sugar is used unless otherwise stated.
● Plain flour is used unless otherwise stated.

OVEN TEMPERATURE CHART

°C	°F	Gas mark
110	225	$\frac{1}{4}$
130	250	$\frac{1}{2}$
140	275	1
150	300	2
170	325	3
180	350	4
190	375	5
200	400	6
220	425	7
230	450	8
240	475	9

KEY TO SYMBOLS

1.00* Indicates minimum preparation and cooking times in hours and minutes. They do not include prepared items in the list of ingredients; calculated times apply only to the method. An asterisk * indicates extra time should be allowed, so check the note below symbols.

Chef's hats indicate degree of difficulty of a recipe: no hat means it is straightforward; one hat slightly more complicated; two hats indicates that it is for more advanced cooks.

£ Indicates a recipe which is good value for money; £ £ indicates an expensive recipe. No £ sign indicates an inexpensive recipe.

✱ Indicates that a recipe will freeze. If there is no symbol, the recipe is unsuitable for freezing. An asterisk * indicates special freezer instructions so check the note immediately below the symbols.

309 cals Indicates calories per serving, including any sugges-tions (e.g. cream, to serve) given in the ingredients.

METRIC CONVERSION SCALE

LIQUID				SOLID		
Imperial	Exact conversion	Recommended ml		Imperial	Exact conversion	Recommended g
$\frac{1}{4}$ pint	142 ml	150 ml		1 oz	28.35 g	25 g
$\frac{1}{2}$ pint	284 ml	300 ml		2 oz	56.7 g	50 g
1 pint	568 ml	600 ml		4 oz	113.4 g	100 g
$1\frac{1}{2}$ pints	851 ml	900 ml		8 oz	226.8 g	225 g
$1\frac{3}{4}$ pints	992 ml	1 litre		12 oz	340.2 g	350 g
For quantities of $1\frac{3}{4}$ pints and over, litres and fractions of a litre have been used.				14 oz	397.0 g	400 g
				16 oz (1 lb)	453.6 g	450 g
				1 kilogram (kg) equals 2.2 lb.		

INDIAN COOKERY

Here, in one volume, is all you will ever need to know about Indian cookery, from everyday snacks and curries to traditional tandoori dishes and exotic feasts for entertaining. Turn the pages of this book and you will quickly see that Indian food is immensely varied, and not necessarily overpowering or hot. Spices are used with subtlety, cream, coconut and yogurt give richness and smoothness to sauces, and nuts and fruits lend texture and sweetness to all kinds of savoury dishes, especially poultry, meat and rice.

The front section of the book is conveniently arranged to follow the Western style of eating, starting with appetisers and main courses, then working through to vegetable and vegetarian dishes, rice and desserts. Every dish is photographed in colour, and there are well over 100 step-by-step illustrations to guide you through cooking methods, plus helpful hints on ingredients and accompaniments, and suggestions for serving.

The back section of the book is an invaluable source of information on Indian cooking. There is a guide to the different styles of cooking in India, with information on specialist equipment, plus recipes for basic breads, accompaniments, yogurt, cheese and drinks, with help on planning an Indian meal, including specimen menus. This adds up to a handy reference section filled with fascinating facts and information, which you will find immensely useful whenever you are cooking Indian food.

Appetisers and Snacks

In this chapter is a selection of starters that you would normally find in an Indian restaurant. Indians rarely eat appetisers or starters. In a traditional Indian meal, all the different dishes are put on the table together and everyone helps themselves to whatever they want. The custom of eating one course at a time has been taken up by Indian restaurants for the sake of their Western customers.

MASALE WALA JHINGA
(BUTTERFLY PRAWNS)

| 0.30* | 🍴 | £ £ | 195 cals |

MEDIUM
* plus 3–4 hours marinating

Serves 4

900 g (2 lb) medium raw prawns, in the shell or 12 raw "jumbo" Mediterranean prawns in the shell

50 g (2 oz) butter

6 garlic cloves, skinned and crushed

juice of 4 limes or 2 lemons

2.5 cm (1 inch) piece of fresh root ginger, peeled and chopped

15 ml (1 tbsp) ground coriander

30 ml (2 tbsp) ground cumin

2.5 ml ($\frac{1}{2}$ tsp) ground cardamom

15 ml (1 tbsp) turmeric

15 ml (1 tbsp) paprika

2.5 ml ($\frac{1}{2}$ tsp) chilli powder

5 ml (1 tsp) salt

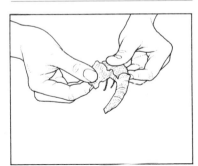

1 Remove the prawn shells, leaving the tail shell intact.

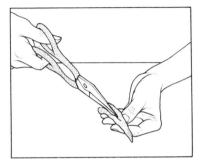

2 Split the prawn along the inner curve, stopping at the tail shell to expose the dark vein.

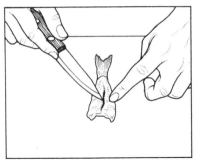

3 Spread the prawn wide open, remove the dark vein and rinse under cold running water. Dry well on absorbent kitchen paper.

4 Melt the butter in a saucepan, then set aside. Put the garlic in a bowl, add the lime or lemon juice, ginger, spices and salt and mix. Stir in melted butter.

5 Coat the prawns with this mixture, cover and marinate in the refrigerator for 3–4 hours.

6 Place the prawns in a grill pan and cook under a preheated hot grill for 2 minutes on each side. Serve immediately, with the juices spooned over, with lime.

Menu Suggestion
Serve this special dish with Nan (Flat Leavened White Bread) page 142 and a chilled dry sparkling white wine or Champagne, and follow with a rich meaty main course such as Shahi Korma (Creamy Lamb and Almond Curry) page 37.

BHOONA JHINGA PURI
(PRAWN CURRY ON PURI)

| 0.40 | ✳* | 315 cals |

MEDIUM-HOT
* freeze the prawn curry only
Serves 6

60 ml (4 tbsp) ghee or vegetable oil

1 medium onion, skinned and finely chopped

2.5 cm (1 inch) piece of fresh root ginger, peeled and crushed

1–2 garlic cloves, skinned and crushed

10 ml (2 tsp) ground coriander

10 ml (2 tsp) ground cumin

5 ml (1 tsp) turmeric

2.5–5 ml (½–1 tsp) chilli powder, according to taste

450 g (1 lb) peeled prawns, defrosted and thoroughly dried if frozen

4 ripe tomatoes, skinned and roughly chopped

30 ml (2 tbsp) vinegar

10 ml (2 tsp) tomato purée

salt

6 uncooked puris (page 142)

vegetable oil, for deep-frying

1 First make the curry. Heat the ghee in a heavy-based frying pan, add the onion, ginger and garlic and fry gently for about 5 minutes until soft and lightly coloured.

2 Add the spices and mix well, then fry for 2 minutes, stirring constantly. Add the prawns, increase the heat and fry for about 5 minutes, stirring all the time to coat in the spice mixture.

3 Add the tomatoes, vinegar, tomato purée and salt to taste. Continue stir-frying until all the liquid has evaporated and the sauce clings thickly to the prawns. Cover the pan, remove from the heat and keep hot.

4 Deep-fry the puris according to the instructions on page 142. Drain, then place 1 puri on each of 6 individual serving plates. Top with the hot prawn curry and serve immediately.

Menu Suggestion
This is a substantial starter and needs no accompaniment other than a chilled dry white wine or lager. Follow with a main course of Tandoori Murgh (Tandoori Chicken) page 60 or Tikka Murgh (Tandoori Chicken Kebabs) page 59 and Rasedar Sabzi (Mixed Vegetable Korma) page 95.

BHOONA JHINGA PURI

The term bhoona, sometimes also spelt bhuna, indicates that the dish is fried on top of the cooker. The ingredients are added gradually, starting with the onion, ginger and garlic (which should be stir fried until the ghee is released); then the spices, and finally the main ingredients. *Bhoona* curries are always made in this way, and the stir frying process should never be hurried. The end result should be a thick coating sauce with a glossy sheen and a full flavour. Always stand over a bhoona curry while it is cooking, and stir the mixture constantly to prevent it sticking to the bottom of the pan. A heavy-based, cast iron or non-stick, frying pan is the best pan to use.

SABZI WALE SAMOSE
(VEGETABLE SAMOSAS)

1.45	🫕 🫕 ✳*	92 cals

MEDIUM-HOT

* freeze before deep-frying

Makes 28

82.5 ml (5½ tbsp) ghee or vegetable oil

1 medium onion, skinned and finely chopped

2 garlic cloves, skinned and crushed

100 g (4 oz) potatoes, scrubbed and finely diced

2 carrots, peeled and finely chopped

10 ml (2 tsp) garam masala (page 140)

10 ml (2 tsp) ground coriander

5 ml (1 tsp) turmeric

2.5–5 ml (½–1 tsp) chilli powder, according to taste

salt

100 g (4 oz) cauliflower florets

50 g (2 oz) frozen peas

225 g (8 oz) plain flour

vegetable oil, for deep-frying

1 First make the filling. Heat 60 ml (4 tbsp) of the ghee in a heavy-based saucepan or flame-proof casserole, add the onion and garlic and fry gently for 5 minutes until soft and lightly coloured.

2 Add the potatoes and carrots and fry gently for 10 minutes, stirring occasionally to coat in the ghee mixture.

3 Add the spices to the potatoes and carrots and mix well, then fry for 2 minutes, stirring constantly.

4 Pour in 900 ml (1½ pints) water, add 5 ml (1 tsp) salt and stir well to mix. Bring to the boil, then simmer uncovered for 15 minutes, stirring occasionally.

5 Meanwhile, divide the cauliflower florets into tiny sprigs, discarding any long or tough stalks. Set aside.

6 Add the cauliflower and peas to the filling mixture and simmer for a further 10 minutes or until the vegetables have absorbed all the liquid and are tender. Remove from the heat, taste and adjust seasoning, then set aside and leave to cool.

7 Make the pastry. Melt and cool the remaining 22.5 ml (1½ tbsp) ghee. Sift the flour and 2.5 ml (½ tsp) salt into a bowl. Work in the ghee with the fingertips.

8 Add 100 ml (3½ fl oz) ice-cold water a little at a time and continue working, with your hands, until a soft dough is formed. Knead for 10 minutes until smooth, then cover with a clean tea towel wrung out in cold water to prevent a crust forming on top. Leave to rest for 15 minutes.

9 Divide the dough in half. Cover one half with the damp tea towel and set aside. Cut the remaining half into 7 equal pieces. Cover them with another damp tea towel.

10 Brush a little vegetable oil on a board or work surface. Roll out 1 piece of dough very thinly to a 10 cm (4 inch) circle. Cut in half.

11 Wet the edges of the semi-circle with water. Place about 5 ml (1 tsp) of the cold filling on the semi-circle, then fold one end of dough in towards the centre.

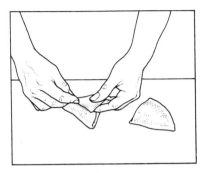

12 Fold the other end of the dough in towards the centre, overlapping it over the first so that it forms a cone shape.

13 Wet the open edges of dough and press to seal. Cover with a damp tea towel. Prepare the remaining samosas in the same way.

14 Heat the oil in a deep-fat fryer to 190°C (375°F). Deep-fry the samosas in batches for 2–3 minutes until golden brown on all sides. Remove with a slotted spoon and drain on absorbent kitchen paper while frying the remainder. Serve hot.

Menu Suggestion

Samosas are eaten with the fingers as a snack food in India, but they also make a delicious starter eaten with a knife and fork. Serve them with a dipping sauce of natural yogurt, finely chopped fresh mint, crushed garlic and salt and pepper. Alternatively, arrange them on a napkin-lined tray or basket and hand them round as a pre-dinner appetizer with drinks.

PIAZ BHAJIAS
(DEEP FRIED ONION FRITTERS)

| 0.15 | £ | 220 cals |

MEDIUM

Serves 4

150 g (5 oz) gram or besan flour (page 135)

5 ml (1 tsp) bicarbonate of soda

10 ml (2 tsp) salt

10 ml (2 tsp) coriander seeds, crushed

2.5 ml ($\frac{1}{2}$ tsp) garam masala (page 140)

5 ml (1 tsp) turmeric

5 ml (1 tsp) chilli powder

4 green cardamoms

30 ml (2 tbsp) chopped fresh mint or coriander (optional)

2 large onions, skinned and chopped

salt and freshly ground pepper

vegetable oil, for deep-frying

lemon or lime wedges, to garnish

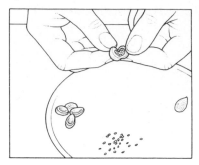

1 Sift the flour, bicarbonate of soda and salt into a bowl. Add the crushed coriander seeds, garam masala, turmeric and chilli powder and mix well.

2 Open the cardamom pods and take out the seeds. Discard the husks and crush the seeds lightly. Add these to the flour mixture together with the mint or coriander (if using), onion, salt and pepper to taste and 30 ml (2 tbsp) water. Mix together thoroughly to a fairly stiff paste.

3 Heat the oil in a deep-fat fryer to 180°C (350°F). Using 2 wet dessertspoons, drop 6 spoonfuls of the mixture into the hot oil and deep-fry the fritters for 3–4 minutes or until darkish brown in colour.

4 Remove from the oil with a slotted spoon and transfer to absorbent kitchen paper to drain. Repeat with the remaining mixture. Serve piping hot, with lemon or lime wedges.

Menu Suggestion
Serve these onion fritters as a starter accompanied by Pudeene Ki Chutney (Mint Chutney) page 149, or serve them as a vegetable accompaniment to any Indian main course.

BHAJIAS
There is often confusion between pakoras and bhajias. In North India they are known as pakoras and served as a teatime snack, in South and West India they are known as bhajias and served as part of a vegetarian main meal.

CHIURA
(BOMBAY MIX)

| 0.40* | 🍴 🍴 £ | 1775 cals |

MEDIUM
* plus 30 minutes soaking and 20
minutes cooling

Makes about 350 g (12 oz)

50 g (2 oz) mung dal (page 137)

50 g (2 oz) toovar dal (page 137)

175 g (6 oz) gram or besan flour
   (page 135)

5 ml (1 tsp) salt

2.5 ml ($\frac{1}{2}$ tsp) ground coriander

2.5 ml ($\frac{1}{2}$ tsp) ground cumin

6.25 ml (1$\frac{1}{4}$ tsp) chilli powder

vegetable oil, for deep-frying

30 ml (2 tbsp) ghee or vegetable oil

50 g (2 oz) natural unsalted
   peanuts

2.5 ml ($\frac{1}{2}$ tsp) turmeric

5 ml (1 tsp) sugar

1 Pick over the dal and remove
any grit or discoloured pulses.
Put into a sieve and wash
thoroughly under cold running
water. Put in a bowl, cover with
cold water and soak 30 minutes.

2 Meanwhile, put the flour in a
bowl, and mix in 2.5 ml ($\frac{1}{2}$ tsp)
of the salt, the coriander, cumin
and 1.25 ml ($\frac{1}{4}$ tsp) of the chilli
powder. Add 60 ml (4 tbsp) cold
water and mix to form a soft
dough. Knead until smooth and
no longer sticky.

3 Heat the oil in a deep-fat fryer
to 180°C (350°F). Put the
dough into a sev-maker (see page
133), potato ricer or sieve.

4 Holding the sev-maker over
the oil, press the dough
through, dropping the 'noodles'
into the oil. Deep-fry for 1–2
minutes until golden brown, then
remove from the oil with a slotted
spoon and drain on absorbent
kitchen paper.

5 Drain the dal and pat
completely dry on absorbent
kitchen paper.

6 Heat the ghee in a frying pan,
add the dals and fry over a
moderate heat for 3–4 minutes.
Add the remaining chilli powder,
peanuts and turmeric and stir-fry
for a further minute. Allow to cool
for 20 minutes.

7 Put the 'noodles' and toasted
dal mixture into a bowl, add
the remaining salt and the sugar
and toss well. Store in an airtight container for up to 3 weeks.

Menu Suggestion
Bombay Mix makes an excellent
"nibble" to hand round with pre-
dinner drinks.

PAPPAR
(POPPADOMS)

| 0.15 | 🎩 | 75 cals |

Serves 4

4 plain or spiced poppadoms
vegetable oil, for frying

Method 1

1 Pour about 1 cm ($\frac{1}{2}$ inch) oil into a large frying pan and put over a medium heat until a crumb or small piece of poppadom will sizzle immediately it is dropped into the oil.

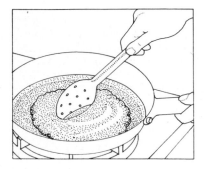

2 Put a poppadom into the oil and cook for a few seconds. It should expand greatly and turn a very pale yellow brown. Do not overcook or let it turn dark brown; if it does, the oil is too hot, so turn down the heat.

3 Remove the poppadom with kitchen tongs and drain on absorbent kitchen paper. Repeat with the remaining poppadoms and serve immediately.

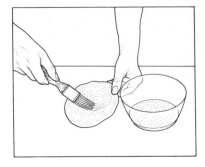

Method 2

1 Preheat a grill, brush each poppadom with a little oil and grill each one for a few seconds on both sides until little bubbles appear and it expands slightly.

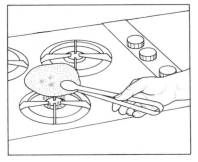

Method 3

1 Brush each poppadom with a little oil. Pick up 1 poppadom with kitchen tongs and hold 1 cm ($\frac{1}{2}$ inch) above a low gas flame. Turn the poppadom quickly as it begins to bubble and brown. Keep turning until the whole poppadom is cooked. Repeat with the remaining poppadoms and serve immediately.

Menu Suggestion

When entertaining in Indian style, offer a tray of crisply fried Poppadoms to your guests with their pre-dinner drinks, or serve them as a light first course.

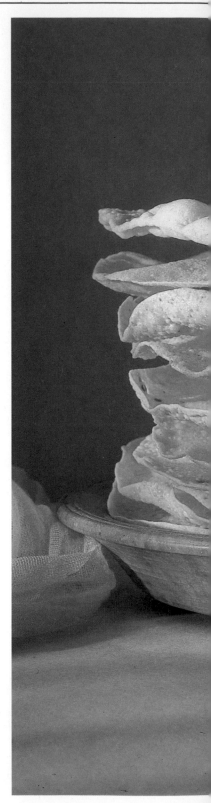

MASALEDAR DAL KA SHORVA
(SPICED DAL SOUP)

| 1.30 | £ | 123–185 cals |

MEDIUM-HOT

Serves 4–6

| 100 g (4 oz) channa dal (page 137) |
| 5 ml (1 tsp) cumin seeds |
| 10 ml (2 tsp) coriander seeds |
| 5 ml (1 tsp) fenugreek seeds |
| 3 dried red chillies |
| 15 ml (1 tbsp) shredded coconut |
| 30 ml (2 tbsp) ghee or vegetable oil |
| 225 g (8 oz) tomatoes, skinned and roughly chopped |
| 2.5 ml (½ tsp) turmeric |
| 15 ml (1 tbsp) tamarind juice (optional — page 141) |
| 5 ml (1 tsp) treacle |
| 5 ml (1 tsp) salt |
| lemon slices and coriander sprigs, to garnish |

1 Pick over the dal and remove any grit or discoloured pulses. Put into a sieve and wash thoroughly under cold running water. Drain well.

2 Place the dal in a large saucepan, cover with 600 ml (1 pint) water and bring to the boil. Cover and simmer for at least 1 hour, or until tender.

3 Finely grind the cumin, coriander, fenugreek, chillies and coconut in a small electric mill or with a pestle and mortar. Heat the ghee in a heavy-based frying pan, add the spice mixture and fry, stirring, for 30 seconds. Set the spices aside.

4 Mash or liquidise the dal and transfer to a large saucepan. Stir in the tomatoes, spices, turmeric, tamarind juice (if using), treacle, salt and a further 300 ml (½ pint) water.

5 Bring to the boil, then lower the heat, cover and simmer for about 20 minutes. Taste and adjust seasoning and turn into a warmed serving dish. Garnish with lemon slices and coriander sprigs and serve immediately.

Menu Suggestion
Serve this spicy soup with crisp Pappar (Poppadoms) page 18 for a first course to an Indian meal. Follow with a main course of Bhoona Gosht (Dry Beef Curry) page 43, Peelay Chaval (Yellow Aromatic Rice) page 108 and Muttar Paneer (Peas with Cheese) page 91.

MASALEDAR DAL KA SHORVA

The shredded coconut in this recipe can be fresh if you want to go to the trouble of preparing a fresh coconut, but for such a small quantity it is more practical to buy ready shredded coconut. It has larger flakes than desiccated coconut, and a fuller flavour. Toasted, it would make an attractive garnish for this soup.

MASALEDAR SHORVA
(MULLIGATAWNY SOUP)

| 2.00 | £ | ✳ | 510 cals |

MILD

Serves 4

900 g (2 lb) neck of lamb

1 medium onion, skinned and chopped

fresh coriander sprig

2.5 ml ($\frac{1}{2}$ tsp) ground mace

50 g (2 oz) ghee or vegetable oil

10 ml (2 tsp) turmeric

5 ml (1 tsp) ground coriander

2.5 ml ($\frac{1}{2}$ tsp) ground cumin

2.5 ml ($\frac{1}{2}$ tsp) ground fenugreek

pinch of cayenne pepper

5 ml (1 tsp) salt

15 ml (1 tbsp) ground rice

coriander sprigs and lemon slices, to garnish

1 Cut the lean flesh from the meat and reserve. Put the rest of the meat with the bones in a large saucepan and add 1.7 litres (3 pints) water, the onion, coriander and mace.

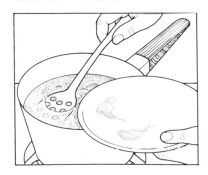

2 Bring to the boil, skimming off the scum that rises to the surface, then simmer for 1 hour or until the meat falls off the bones.

3 Strain the liquid into a bowl and set aside. Reserve the cooked meat and discard bones.

4 Heat the ghee in a clean saucepan and add the reserved raw and cooked meat, the turmeric, coriander, cumin, fenugreek, cayenne and salt. Cook gently for 5 minutes or until the juices run from the meat, then add the strained stock and continue to simmer for 20 minutes until the meat is quite tender.

5 Mix the ground rice with 30 ml (2 tbsp) cold water until smooth. Gradually add this to the soup, stirring constantly. Bring to the boil, then lower the heat and simmer for a further 15 minutes. Taste and adjust seasoning before serving. Serve hot, garnished with coriander sprigs and lemon slices.

Menu Suggestion

Peppery hot Mulligatawny Soup tastes good with Pappar (Poppadoms) page 18. Follow with a main course of Gosht Aur Aloocha (Pork Chops with Plums) page 56 and a vegetable dish such as Tale Hua Masaledar Aloo (Fried Masala Potatoes) page 85.

MASALEDAR SHORVA

Literally translated mulligatawny means "pepper water". The recipe originated in the days of the Raj. Although the soup course did not exist in an Indian meal, British army officers in India insisted on soup being served; mulligatawny was invented to keep them happy.

Seekh Kebab
(SPICY MINCED LAMB KEBABS)

| 0.40 | 🍴 | ✳* | 195 cals |

MEDIUM

* freeze before cooking at the end of step 4

Serves 4

10 ml (2 tsp) coriander seeds

10 ml (2 tsp) cumin seeds

4 whole cloves

seeds of 4 green cardamoms

few black peppercorns

2 garlic cloves, skinned and roughly chopped

1 fresh green or red chilli, seeded and roughly chopped

coarse sea salt

450 g (1 lb) raw finely minced lamb (eg fillet or shoulder)

1 small onion, skinned and grated

30 ml (2 tbsp) chopped fresh coriander

15 ml (1 tbsp) lemon juice

vegetable oil, for brushing

1 Dry fry the coriander and cumin seeds in a heavy-based frying pan with the cloves, cardamom seeds and peppercorns.

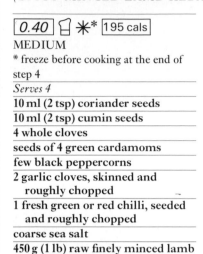

2 Turn the dry-fried spices into a mortar. Add the garlic, chilli and 5 ml (1 tsp) salt and pound well with a pestle. Alternatively, grind in a small electric mill.

3 Put the lamb in a bowl and add the onion, pounded spice mixture, fresh coriander and lemon juice. Mix with your hands, squeezing the mixture well so that it clings together.

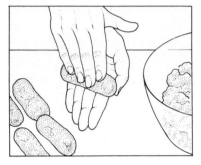

4 Divide the mixture into 16 equal pieces. With wetted hands, roll the spiced meat into sausage shapes.

5 Thread 4 kebabs on to each of 4 oiled flat kebab skewers. Brush with oil, then barbecue or grill for 5–8 minutes, turning frequently until sizzling and well browned on all sides. Serve hot.

Menu Suggestion

Serve as a dinner party starter, with wedges of lemon and thinly sliced rings of raw onion. For the main course, Sufaid Murgh (Chicken Cooked in Coconut Milk) page 62 and Sag Aloo (Spinach and Potatoes) page 86 would make a good combination.

Shami Kebab
(SPICY MEAT AND LENTIL PATTIES)

| 1.30* | £ | ✳ | 315 cals |

MEDIUM-HOT

* plus 2 hours cooling and 30 minutes chilling

Serves 6

175 g (6 oz) masoor dal (page 137)

450 g (1 lb) raw minced lamb or beef

4 garlic cloves, skinned and crushed

1 medium onion, skinned and finely minced

2.5 cm (1 inch) piece of fresh root ginger, peeled and finely chopped

2 small fresh green chillies, seeded and finely chopped

5 ml (1 tsp) ground cumin

5 ml (1 tsp) ground coriander

5 ml (1 tsp) salt

8 black peppercorns

45 ml (3 tbsp) chopped fresh mint

50 g (2 oz) butter, softened

2 eggs, beaten

little ghee or oil, for frying

lemon or lime wedges, to serve

1 Put the masoor dal in a large saucepan with the minced meat, garlic, onion, ginger, chopped chillies, cumin, coriander, salt, peppercorns, half of the chopped mint and 450 ml ($\frac{3}{4}$ pint) water.

2 Bring to the boil, then lower the heat and simmer, uncovered, for at least 45 minutes or until the masoor dal is tender and most of the water is absorbed. Stir the mixture frequently during cooking to prevent it sticking. When cooked, turn the mixture into a bowl and cool completely, for at least 2 hours.

3 Place the cold mixture in a blender or food processor with the softened butter, the remaining mint and eggs. Work until smooth and well amalgamated, then tip out on to a plate or board.

5 Wipe a heavy-based frying pan with a little ghee and put over a moderate heat until hot. Cook the kebabs in batches for 3 minutes on each side until crisp and golden brown. Do not try to move the kebabs while they cook or they will disintegrate.

6 Serve these spicy meat and lentil patties hot, garnished with lemon or lime wedges.

4 Wetting your hand to prevent the mixture sticking, shape the mixture into 24 small round flat cakes, place on greaseproof paper. Chill for 30 minutes.

Menu Suggestion
Serve for a starter or a tasty snack accompanied by a refreshing Raita (Cucumber with Yogurt) page 152 or Pudeene Ki Chutney (Mint Chutney) page 149.

SEEKH AND SHAMI KEBABS
In India, kebabs such as these can be bought from street stalls. Although restaurants serve them as starters or main courses, kebabs are really snack foods to be eaten with the fingers, sometimes wrapped in bread.

Lamb, Beef and Pork

Hindus cannot eat beef and Muslims cannot eat pork, therefore lamb is the most popular meat in Indian cookery. There is no reason why you should not substitute beef for lamb, or vice versa. Provided you use a suitable cut, all three meats are interchangeable. Cooking methods too can be altered: curries can be cooked on top of the cooker or in the oven; the method in each recipe is only one suggestion.

RAAN
(SPICED LEG OF LAMB)

2.15* £ £ 770 cals

MEDIUM

* plus 12 hours marinating

Serves 6

2 medium onions, skinned and
    roughly chopped

6 garlic cloves, skinned and
    roughly chopped

5 cm (2 inch) piece of fresh root
    ginger, peeled and chopped

75 g (3 oz) whole blanched
    almonds

5 cm (2 inch) stick cinnamon

10 green cardamoms

4 whole cloves

5 ml (1 tsp) aniseed seeds

30 ml (2 tbsp) cumin seeds

15 ml (1 tbsp) ground coriander

2.5 ml ($\frac{1}{2}$ tsp) grated nutmeg

10 ml (2 tsp) turmeric

10 ml (2 tsp) chilli powder

10 ml (2 tsp) salt

30 ml (2 tbsp) lemon or lime juice

600 ml (1 pint) natural yogurt

2.3 kg (5 lb) leg of lamb

25 g (1 oz) blanched slivered
    almonds

50 g (2 oz) sultanas

1 Place all the ingredients except
the lamb, slivered almonds
and sultanas in a blender or food
processor and work until smooth.

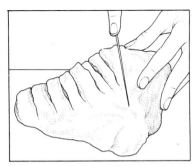

2 Remove all the fat and white
membrane from the lamb.
With a sharp knife, make deep
slashes all over the meat through
to the bone.

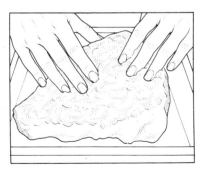

3 Rub one-third of the yogurt
mixture well into the lamb and
place in an ovenproof baking dish
or casserole. Pour the remaining
yogurt mixture over the top of the
meat and around the sides. Cover
and leave to marinate in the
refrigerator for 12 hours.

4 Allow the dish to come to
room temperature, then cover
tightly with the lid or foil. Bake in
the oven at 180°C (350°F) mark 4
for 1$\frac{1}{4}$ hours, then uncover and
bake for a further 45 minutes,
basting occasionally, or until the
lamb is completely tender.

5 Transfer the lamb to a warmed
serving dish, pour the sauce
around the meat and scatter the
almonds and sultanas over the top.
Serve hot.

Menu Suggestion
Serve for a dinner party main
course or for an unusual Sunday
lunch, with Peelay Chaval (Yellow
Aromatic Rice) page 108 and Hare
Sem Aur Nariyal (Green Beans
with Coconut) page 89.

GOSHT BIRYANI
(SPICED LAMB AND RICE CASSEROLE)

| 2.00 | 🍴 | f | 710 cals |

MILD

Serves 6

450 g (1 lb) basmati rice

1 medium onion, skinned and roughly chopped

2 garlic cloves, skinned

2.5 cm (1 inch) piece of fresh root ginger, peeled and roughly chopped

150 ml (¼ pint) ghee or vegetable oil

450 g (1 lb) boned shoulder of lamb, trimmed of excess fat and cut into 2.5 cm (1 inch) cubes

150 ml (¼ pint) natural yogurt

50 g (2 oz) ground almonds

4 whole cloves

2 black cardamoms

4 green cardamoms

5 ml (1 tsp) cumin seeds

2.5 cm (1 inch) stick cinnamon or 4 pieces of cassia bark

50 g (2 oz) sultanas

5–10 ml (1–2 tsp) salt

large pinch of saffron threads, or 5 ml (1 tsp) each yellow and orange food colourings

5 ml (1 tsp) rose water

Bhuni Hui Piaz (Crisp Browned Onions) page 152, to garnish

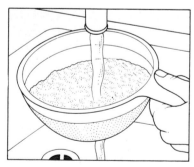

1 Put the rice in a sieve and wash well under cold running water until the water runs clear. Transfer the rice to a bowl, cover with cold water and leave to soak.

2 Meanwhile, put the onion, garlic and ginger in a blender or food processor and work until smooth. Set aside.

3 Heat 60 ml (4 tbsp) of the ghee in a large flameproof casserole. Add the cubes of lamb and fry over high heat until well browned on all sides. Transfer to a plate with a slotted spoon.

4 Add the onion purée to the residual ghee in the pan and fry over high heat for 2 minutes, stirring constantly. Return the meat to the pan, then stir in the yogurt 1 spoonful at a time. Cook each addition over high heat, stirring constantly, until the yogurt is absorbed.

5 Add the ground almonds and 150 ml (¼ pint) water. Bring to the boil, cover and simmer gently for 30 minutes, stirring occasionally to prevent sticking.

6 Heat another 60 ml (4 tbsp) ghee in a large heavy-based frying pan, add the cloves, cardamom pods, cumin seeds and cinnamon and fry gently for 1 minute.

7 Drain the rice well and add to the spices, stirring until the rice absorbs all the fat. Stir in the sultanas and salt to taste.

8 Sprinkle the spiced rice evenly over the meat in the casserole. Carefully pour in enough water to just cover the rice. DO NOT STIR. Bring to the boil, cover and bake in the oven at 150°C (300°F) mark 2 for 30 minutes.

9 Meanwhile, if using saffron threads, soak them in 60 ml (4 tbsp) boiling water.

10 Remove the casserole from the oven, uncover and drizzle over the saffron water or food colourings. Recover tightly and bake for 15 minutes.

11 To serve, uncover the biryani and carefully fork up the meat and rice. Sprinkle with the rose water and, finally, the onion garnish.

Menu Suggestion

Serve for an informal supper party, with Tamatar Aur Diaz Ki Chutney (Tomato and Onion Chutney) page 148, Raita (Cucumber with Yogurt) page 152 and quartered hard-boiled eggs.

ROGAN JOSH
(RED LAMB OR BEEF CURRY WITH PEPPERS AND TOMATOES)

2.15   ✳*   650 cals

MEDIUM

* freeze without the pepper, tomato and yogurt garnish

Serves 4

75 ml (3 fl oz) ghee or vegetable oil

2 medium onions, skinned and thinly sliced

1 large garlic clove, skinned and crushed

2.5 cm (1 inch) piece of fresh root ginger, peeled and crushed or finely chopped

4 green cardamoms, crushed

10 ml (2 tsp) turmeric

10 ml (2 tsp) ground coriander

10 ml (2 tsp) ground cumin

10 ml (2 tsp) paprika

2.5 ml ($\frac{1}{2}$ tsp) chilli powder

900 g (2 lb) lamb fillet or chuck steak, trimmed of excess fat and cut into cubes

1 red pepper

1 green pepper

6 ripe tomatoes, skinned

300 ml ($\frac{1}{2}$ pint) natural yogurt

salt

1   Heat 50 ml (2 fl oz) of the ghee in a heavy-based saucepan or flameproof casserole, add the onion, garlic and ginger and fry gently for about 5 minutes until soft and lightly coloured.

2   Add the spices and fry gently for 2 minutes, stirring constantly. Increase the heat to moderate, add the meat in batches and fry until browned on all sides.

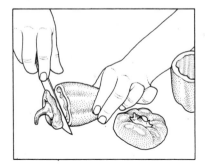

3   Cut off the tops of the peppers, slice in half lengthways then remove and discard the cores and seeds.

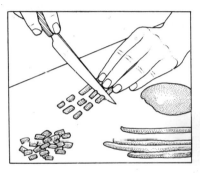

4   Chop half of the red pepper and half of the green pepper finely. Slice the other two halves into thin strips. Chop 4 of the tomatoes.

5   Reserve about 60 ml (4 tbsp) of the yogurt. Add the remainder to the pan, 15 ml (1 tbsp) at a time. Cook each addition over high heat, stirring constantly, until the yogurt is absorbed. Sprinkle in salt to taste.

6   Add the chopped red and green pepper and tomatoes to the meat, increase the heat and fry until the juices run, stirring and tossing the contents of the pan all the time.

7   Put a double thickness of foil over the top of the pan and seal tightly with the lid. Simmer gently for about 1$\frac{1}{2}$ hours until the meat is tender. Check the contents of the pan every 30 minutes or so and stir well to prevent sticking.

8   Before serving, heat the remaining ghee in a frying pan, add the red and green pepper strips and fry over gentle heat for a few minutes until softened. Add the remaining chopped tomatoes with a pinch of salt, increase the heat and toss vigorously to combine with the peppers.

9   When the curry is ready to serve, turn into a warmed serving dish and spoon the pepper and tomato mixture on top. Drizzle over the remaining yogurt and serve immediately.

Menu Suggestion
Rogan Josh makes an attractive and tasty main course dish for a supper party. Serve with Sag Aloo (Spinach and Potatoes) page 86 and Phool Gobi Ki Bhaji (Cauliflower in Curry Sauce) page 92.

MHAANS MUGHLAI
(MUGHLAI LAMB WITH TURNIPS)

| 2.30 | ✳ | 599 cals |

MEDIUM-HOT

Serves 4

2.5 cm (1 inch) piece of fresh root
   ginger, peeled and roughly
   chopped

30 ml (2 tbsp) coriander seeds

7.5 ml (1½ tsp) poppy seeds

30 ml (2 tbsp) desiccated coconut

2 dried red chillies, crushed

50 ml (2 fl oz) ghee

1 large onion, skinned and thinly
   sliced

5 ml (1 tsp) paprika

900 g (2 lb) lamb fillet, trimmed of
   excess fat and cut into cubes

50 ml (2 fl oz) natural yogurt

10 ml (2 tsp) tomato purée

10 ml (2 tsp) turmeric

5 ml (1 tsp) salt

450 g (1 lb) small young turnips,
   peeled and halved or cut into
   large chunks

1 Finely grind the ginger,
coriander and poppy seeds,
desiccated coconut and chillies in
a small electric mill or a pestle and
mortar.

2 Heat the ghee in a heavy-based
saucepan or flameproof
casserole, add the onion and
paprika and fry gently, stirring
frequently, for about 10 minutes
until softened. Remove with a
slotted spoon and set aside.

3 Add the meat to the residual
ghee in batches and fry over
moderate heat until well browned
on all sides. Add the yogurt and
tomato purée and fry, stirring, for
a few minutes more until
thickened.

4 Add the ground spice mixture,
the turmeric and salt, then add
the turnips and return the onion to
the pan. Fry for 2 minutes, stirring well and tossing the
ingredients in the pan so that they
become well combined.

5 Pour in 150 ml (¼ pint) water
and stir well to combine. Bring
to the boil, then simmer for about
15 minutes until the sauce is thick
and reduced, stirring frequently.

6 Add another 150 ml (¼ pint)
water and repeat the simmering and stirring process as in
step 5 above.

7 Add 300 ml (½ pint) water and
bring to simmering point, stirring. Cover the pan and simmer
gently for about 1½ hours, or until
the lamb is very tender.

8 Increase the heat to high and
stir until all the sauce has
reduced and is just clinging to the
meat and turnips. Turn into a
warmed serving dish.

Menu Suggestion
Serve for a substantial family meal
with Masaledal Basmati (Spiced
Fried Basmati Rice) page 107 and
a refreshing Raita (Cucumber with
Yogurt) page 152.

MHAANS MUGHLAI
Any dish called mughlai is rich
in ghee and spices, and this
recipe for mughlai lamb is no
exception. Mughlai dishes come
from southern India, from the
state of Andhra Pradesh, in
which the city of Hyderabad is
famous for its sumptuously rich
cooking. Look for mughlai
dishes on Indian restaurant
menus: they are often in a
separate section, as they are
regarded as being very special.

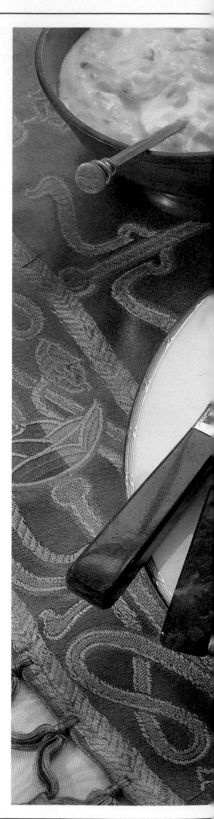

SHAKOTEE
(CURRIED LAMB WITH COCONUT)

MEDIUM-HOT

* freeze without the spiced coconut garnish

Serves 4

1 fresh coconut

15 ml (1 tbsp) poppy seeds

15 ml (1 tbsp) cumin seeds

15 ml (1 tbsp) black peppercorns

5 cm (2 inch) stick cinnamon, broken into short pieces

4 whole cloves

2 dried red chillies, roughly chopped

90 ml (6 tbsp) ghee or vegetable oil

2 medium onions, skinned and finely chopped

3 garlic cloves, skinned and crushed

1 cm ($\frac{1}{2}$ inch) piece of fresh root ginger, peeled and very finely chopped

900 g (2 lb) lamb fillet, trimmed of excess fat and cut into cubes

5 ml (1 tsp) turmeric

5 ml (1 tsp) salt

1.25 ml ($\frac{1}{4}$ tsp) grated nutmeg

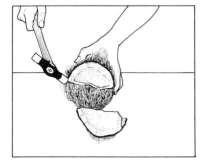

1 Drain off the coconut milk. Hit the coconut sharply with a mallet or small hammer, then tap all the way round until the shell falls apart in several pieces.

2 With a sharp, pointed knife, dig out the coconut flesh from the shell. Grate it by hand on a conical or box grater, or work in a food processor.

3 Put two-thirds of the grated coconut in a bowl, pour in 600 ml (1 pint) boiling water and stir well. Cover and leave to stand while preparing the remaining ingredients.

4 Put the poppy and cumin seeds in a heavy-based frying pan with the peppercorns, cinnamon, cloves and chillies. Dry fry for a few minutes, stirring all the time, then turn into a small electric mill or pestle and mortar. Grind the spices, then transfer them to a bowl.

5 Add the remaining grated coconut to the pan and dry fry until lightly browned, tossing and stirring constantly. (You may have to do this in batches, depending on the size of frying pan used.) Add to the spices in the bowl and stir well to mix.

6 Heat 60 ml (4 tbsp) of the ghee in a heavy-based saucepan or flameproof casserole, add the onions, garlic and ginger and fry gently for about 5 minutes until soft and lightly coloured.

7 Add the meat in batches and fry over moderate heat until well browned on all sides, then add two-thirds of the coconut and spice mixture, the turmeric, salt and nutmeg. Fry for a few minutes more, tossing and stirring the contents of the pan so that the ingredients combine evenly.

8 Strain in the coconut milk and bring to the boil, stirring. Lower the heat, cover and simmer gently for 1$\frac{1}{2}$ hours or until the meat is tender. Stir frequently during this time, to prevent sticking.

9 Before serving, heat the remaining ghee in a frying pan until smoking hot. Add the remaining coconut and spice mixture and toss over high heat until golden brown. Turn the curry into a warmed serving dish and scatter the coconut mixture over the top. Serve hot.

Menu Suggestion

The coconut in Shakotee makes it a rich and creamy dish, perfect for entertaining. Serve with a contrasting accompaniment such as Uble Chaval (Plain Boiled Rice) page 109 or Piaz Aur Hari Mirch Wali Bhindi (Okra Fried with Onion and Green Chilli) page 88.

GOSHT DHANSAK
(SPICY LAMB WITH VEGETABLES AND PULSES)

 £ ✳ 570 cals

HOT

Serves 6

60 ml (4 tbsp) ghee or vegetable oil

900 g (2 lb) shoulder of lamb, trimmed of excess fat and cut into 2.5 cm (1 inch) cubes

2 garlic cloves, skinned and crushed

2.5 cm (1 inch) piece of fresh root ginger, peeled and finely chopped

75 g (3 oz) channa dal (page 137)

75 g (3 oz) masoor dal (page 137)

75 g (3 oz) toovar dal (page 137)

1 small aubergine, cut into 2.5 cm (1 inch) cubes

225 g (8 oz) pumpkin, marrow or courgettes, cut into 2.5 cm (1 inch) cubes

4 tomatoes, skinned and roughly chopped

1 small fresh green chilli

5 ml (1 tsp) turmeric

10 ml (2 tsp) salt

30 ml (2 tbsp) chopped fresh mint or coriander or 10 ml (2 tsp) dried mint

2.5 cm (1 inch) stick cinnamon, lightly crushed

6 green cardamoms

4 whole cloves

10 ml (2 tsp) coriander seeds

10 ml (2 tsp) cumin seeds

10 black peppercorns

2 dried red chillies

chopped fresh coriander and Bhuni Hui Piaz (Crisp Browned Onions) page 152, to garnish

1 Heat the ghee in a large heavy-based saucepan or flameproof casserole, add the meat in batches and fry over high heat until well browned on all sides. Transfer to a plate with a slotted spoon.

2 Add the garlic and ginger to the residual ghee and fry gently for 1 minute or until just turning golden. Return the meat to the pan and then remove from the heat.

3 Pick over the dals and remove any grit or discoloured pulses. Put into a sieve and wash thoroughly under cold running water. Drain well.

4 Add the dals to the saucepan with the aubergine, pumpkin and tomatoes. Stir well to mix.

5 Cut the green chilli in half and remove the seeds. Chop the flesh finely and add to the pan with the turmeric, salt and chopped fresh mint.

6 Pour in enough water to just cover the meat and vegetables, stir well and gradually bring to the boil. Lower the heat, cover tightly and simmer gently for about 1 hour, stirring occasionally. Check from time to time that there is enough liquid in the pan to prevent the dhansak catching.

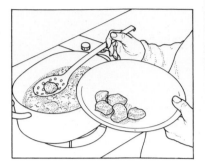

7 After 1 hour, remove the pieces of meat from the pan and set aside. Place the dal and vegetable mixture in a blender or food processor and work until smooth. Alternatively, leave the meat in the sauce and stir well to break up the dal and vegetables. This will give a chunkier texture to the sauce.

8 Put the cinnamon, cardamom pods, cloves, coriander, cumin, peppercorns and chillies into a small electric grinder or blender with 45 ml (3 tbsp) water and blend to a smooth mixture (masala).

9 Return the meat to the pan and pour over the vegetable and dal sauce. Stir in the masala. Cover and simmer for a further 15 minutes or until the meat is tender.

10 To serve, transfer to a warmed serving dish and garnish with chopped fresh coriander and onions. Serve immediately.

Menu Suggestion
This lamb dish is cooked with its own vegetables and pulses, therefore only plain accompaniments are needed to make a substantial main course. Serve with Uble Chaval (Plain Boiled Rice) page 109 and Nan (Flat Leavened White Bread) page 142.

SHAHI KORMA
(CREAMY LAMB AND ALMOND CURRY)

| 1.40 | £ £ ✳* | 745–1025 cals |

MILD

* freeze at the end of step 3

Serves 4–6

100 ml (4 fl oz) ghee or butter

1 large onion, skinned and thinly
    sliced

1–2 garlic cloves, skinned and
    crushed

2.5 cm (1 inch) piece of fresh root
    ginger, peeled and very finely
    chopped or crushed

15 ml (1 tbsp) coriander seeds

10 ml (2 tsp) whole cloves

10 ml (2 tsp) black peppercorns

6 green cardamoms

900 g–1.1 kg (2–2½ lb) boneless
    lamb fillet, trimmed of excess
    fat and cut into cubes

10 ml (2 tsp) turmeric

finely grated rind and juice of
    1 lime or lemon

50 g (2 oz) ground almonds

salt

200 ml (7 fl oz) double cream

25–50 g (1–2 oz) flaked blanched
    almonds

grated lemon or lime rind,
    to garnish

1 Heat the ghee in a heavy-based
saucepan or flameproof
casserole, add the onion, garlic
and ginger and fry very gently,
stirring frequently, for about 10
minutes until soft and lightly
coloured.

2 Meanwhile, finely grind the
coriander seeds, cloves,
peppercorns and cardamoms in a
small electric mill or with a pestle
and mortar. Add to the pan and
stir well to mix. Fry for 1–2
minutes, stirring all the time.

3 Increase the heat and add the
lamb to the casserole a few
pieces at a time. Fry until well
browned on all sides before adding
the next batch. Stir in the
turmeric, lime or lemon juice and
ground almonds, then add salt to
taste. Cover the pan and simmer
gently for 45 minutes to 1 hour
until the lamb is tender.

4 Slowly stir the cream into the
casserole, then heat through.
Taste and adjust seasoning, then
turn into a warmed serving dish.
Sprinkle with the flaked almonds
and the grated lime or lemon rind
and serve immediately.

Menu uggestion
A rich and creamy dish, best
reserved for a special occasion
meal. Serve with Chapatis
(Unleavened Wholemeal Bread)
page 144) and Hare Sem Aur
Nariyal (Green Beans with
Coconut) page 89 or Sag Aloo
(Spinach and Potatoes) page 86.

SHAHI KORMA
As you might expect, the term
shahi refers to a very special
dish fit for a shah or emperor.
Often the word is translated as
"royal", and the recipe usually
contains rich ingredients such
as cream and almonds. Shahi
dishes invariably come from
southern India, particularly
Hyderabad.

SAG GOSHT
(BEEF AND SPINACH CURRY)

| 2.00 | 🍴 | £ | ✳ | 407–611 cals |

MEDIUM-HOT

Serves 4–6

10 black peppercorns

4 cloves

2 bay leaves

seeds of 6 cardamoms

10 ml (2 tsp) cumin seeds

15 ml (1 tbsp) coriander seeds

2.5 ml ($\frac{1}{2}$ tsp) chilli powder

5 ml (1 tsp) salt

900 g (2 lb) lean stewing beef

90 ml (6 tbsp) ghee or vegetable oil

1 large onion, skinned and finely
chopped

6 garlic cloves, skinned and
crushed

2.5 cm (1 inch) piece of fresh root
ginger, peeled and finely
chopped

150 ml ($\frac{1}{4}$ pint) natural yogurt

900 g (2 lb) fresh spinach, stalks
removed and washed
thoroughly, or two 300 g (10.6 oz)
packets frozen spinach, thawed
and drained

1 Finely grind the peppercorns,
cloves, bay leaves, cardamom,
cumin and coriander seeds, chilli
powder and salt in a small electric
mill with a pestle and mortar.

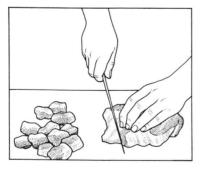

2 Trim the beef, cutting away
any fat. Cut the meat into
2.5 cm (1 inch) pieces.

3 Heat the ghee in a large heavy-
based saucepan or flameproof
casserole, add the onion, garlic,
ginger and ground spices and cook
over moderate heat for about 5
minutes until softened and just
turning brown.

4 Increase the heat and add the
meat. Cook, stirring all the
time, until the meat is well
browned on all sides. Add the
yogurt to the pan, 15 ml (1 tbsp) at
a time. Cook each addition over
high heat, stirring constantly, until
the yogurt is absorbed.

5 Cover the pan tightly with a
lid and turn down the heat to
very low. Simmer, stirring
occasionally, for 1$\frac{1}{2}$ hours or until
the meat is tender.

6 Add the spinach, mix well and
cook over moderate heat for a
further 5–10 minutes, stirring all
the time until the liquid has
evaporated. Taste and adjust
seasoning before serving.

Menu Suggestion
Serve for a 'midweek special'
family meal. Masaledal Basmati
(Spiced Fried Basmati Rice) page
107 makes a good accompaniment,
with Raita (Cucumber with
Yogurt) page 152.

KHUMBI AUR GOSHT
(BEEF AND MUSHROOM CURRY)

| 2.15 | ✳ | 520 cals |

MEDIUM

Serves 4

60 ml (4 tbsp) ghee or vegetable oil

1 onion, skinned and finely chopped

1–2 garlic cloves, skinned and crushed

15 ml (1 tbsp) ground coriander

10 ml (2 tsp) garam masala (page 140)

2.5–5 ml ($\frac{1}{2}$–1 tsp) chilli powder, according to taste

30 ml (2 tbsp) natural yogurt or milk

900 g (2 lb) stewing beef, trimmed of excess fat and cut into large cubes

30 ml (2 tbsp) plain flour

salt

225 g (8 oz) mushrooms, wiped

30 ml (2 tbsp) chopped fresh coriander, to garnish

1 Heat 45 ml (3 tbsp) of the ghee in a heavy-based saucepan or flameproof casserole, add the onion and garlic and fry gently for about 5 minutes until soft and lightly coloured.

2 Meanwhile, mix the spices to a paste with the yogurt or milk. Add the beef to the casserole, a few pieces at a time, and fry until well browned on all sides.

3 Add the spice paste and flour and fry for a further 5 minutes, stirring and tossing the meat so that it becomes well coated in the spices.

4 Pour in 450 ml ($\frac{3}{4}$ pint) water, add 5 ml (1 tsp) salt and bring to the boil, stirring. Lower the heat, cover and simmer gently for $1\frac{1}{2}$–2 hours until the beef is just tender, stirring occasionally.

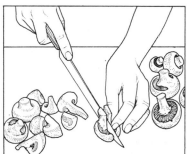

5 Halve or slice the mushrooms if large. Heat the remaining ghee in a frying pan, add the mushrooms and fry over brisk heat, tossing them constantly until they are lightly coloured on all sides. With a slotted spoon, transfer to the pan or casserole. Continue cooking for a further 30 minutes until the beef is tender.

6 Before serving, stir in half of the fresh coriander and taste and adjust seasoning. Turn into a warmed serving dish, sprinkle with the remaining coriander and serve hot.

Menu Suggestion
For a family meal, this curry makes a tasty alternative to a traditional stew or casserole. Serve with Uble Chaval (Plain Boiled Rice) page 109 and a vegetable dish such as Hare Sem Aur Nariyal (Green Beans with Coconut) page 89.

GOSHT MADRASI
(BEEF MADRAS)

2.00	£	343–514 cals

HOT

Serves 4–6

7.5 ml (1½ tsp) chilli powder

10 ml (2 tsp) ground coriander

10 ml (2 tsp) turmeric

1.25 ml (¼ tsp) ground ginger

1.25 ml (¼ tsp) ground pepper

300 ml (½ pint) coconut milk (page 134)

60 ml (4 tbsp) ghee or vegetable oil

2 medium onions, skinned and chopped

2 garlic cloves, skinned and crushed

900 g (2 lb) lean stewing beef, trimmed and cut into 2.5 cm (1 inch) cubes

300 ml (½ pint) beef stock

lemon juice

salt

1 Mix the spices and pepper to a paste with a little of the coconut milk. Set aside.

2 Heat the ghee in a large, heavy-based saucepan or flameproof casserole, add the onion and garlic and fry gently for about 5 minutes until soft and lightly coloured. Add the spicy paste and fry, stirring constantly, for another 3–4 minutes.

3 Add the meat and stock and bring slowly to the boil. Cover and simmer gently for about 1½ hours or until tender.

4 Add the remaining coconut milk, with lemon juice and salt to taste. Bring to the boil, lower the heat and simmer for 8–10 minutes until slightly thickened.

Menu Suggestion
Serve with Uble Chaval (Plain Boiled Rice) page 109 and Pappar (Poppadoms) page 18. Neebu Ka Achar (Lime Pickle) page 149 and Sag Aloo (Spinach and Potatoes) page 86 would also go well.

DUM GOSHT
(BEEF CURRY WITH YOGURT)

2.00	✳	535 cals

HOT

Serves 4

50 ml (2 fl oz) ghee or vegetable oil

900 g (2 lb) chuck steak, trimmed of excess fat and cut into large cubes

2 green chillies

2 medium onions, skinned and finely chopped

225 g (8 oz) tomatoes, skinned and roughly chopped

10 ml (2 tsp) garam masala (page 140)

5 ml (1 tsp) ground ginger

2.5 ml ($\frac{1}{2}$ tsp) cayenne pepper

salt and freshly ground pepper

300 ml ($\frac{1}{2}$ pint) natural yogurt

1 Heat the ghee in a heavy flame-proof casserole, add the beef in batches and fry over high heat until well browned on all sides. Remove with a slotted spoon and drain on absorbent kitchen paper.

2 Meanwhile, discard the ends of the chillies and slice them in half lengthways. Scoop out the seeds. Chop the flesh finely, adding as many seeds as you like—the more you add, the hotter the curry.

3 Add the onions and chillies to the residual ghee, lower the heat and fry gently for about 10 minutes until softened. Add the tomatoes, increase the heat and fry, stirring, for about 5 minutes.

4 Add the spices, with salt and pepper to taste, and fry for 1–2 minutes, stirring. Return the beef to the casserole and mix well.

5 Reserve about 60 ml (4 tbsp) of the yogurt. Add the remainder to the beef, 15 ml (1 tbsp) at a time. Cook each addition over high heat, stirring constantly, until the yogurt is absorbed.

6 When all the yogurt has been added, put a double thickness of foil over the top of the casserole, then seal tightly with the lid.

7 Bake in the oven at 170°C (325°F) mark 3 for 1$\frac{1}{2}$ hours, without lifting the lid. Serve hot in a warmed serving dish, with the reserved yogurt drizzled over.

Menu Suggestion

This thick, dry curry needs to be served with colourful vegetable dishes. Piaz Aur Hari Mirch Wali Bhindi (Okra Fried with Onion and Green Chilli) page 88 would be suitable, or Muttar Paneer (Peas with Cheese) page 91. Chapatis (Unleavened Wholemeal Bread) page 144 or Parathas (Shallow-fried Unleavened Wholemeal Bread) page 144 could also be served instead of, or as well as, Uble Chaval (Plain Boiled Rice) page 109.

BHOONA GOSHT
(DRY BEEF CURRY)

| 1.30 | 🝙 | ✳* | 626 cals |

MEDIUM

* freeze without the yogurt garnish

Serves 4

900 g (2 lb) chuck steak, trimmed
    of excess fat

75 ml (3 fl oz) ghee or vegetable oil

1 small onion, skinned and thinly
    sliced

2 garlic cloves, skinned and
    roughly chopped

1 cm ($\frac{1}{2}$ inch) piece of fresh root
    ginger, peeled and finely
    chopped

5 ml (1 tsp) chilli powder

10 ml (2 tsp) ground cumin

5 ml (1 tsp) ground coriander

7.5 ml (1$\frac{1}{2}$ tsp) garam masala
    (page 140)

10 ml (2 tsp) vinegar

5 ml (1 tsp) salt

60 ml (4 tbsp) desiccated coconut,
    to finish

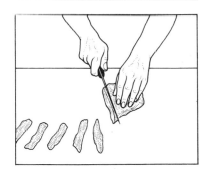

1 Cut the steak into thin slivers.
Heat the ghee in a large heavy-
based frying pan, add the steak
and fry over high heat, shaking the
pan and tossing the meat so that it
becomes well browned on all
sides. Remove with a slotted
spoon and set aside on a plate.

2 Lower the heat under the pan
and add the onion, garlic and
ginger. Fry gently, stirring
frequently, for about 5 minutes
until softened, then add the spices
and fry for a further 2 minutes,
stirring.

3 Return the beef to the pan
with the juices that have
collected on the plate. Mix well
with the onion and spice mixture,
then sprinkle the vinegar and salt
into the pan.

4 Cook, uncovered, over low
heat for about 1 hour or until
the meat is tender. Stir as often as
possible during the cooking time,
to prevent the meat sticking to the
bottom of the pan.

5 Before serving, sprinkle in half
of the desiccated coconut and
stir until all the liquid is absorbed,
raising the heat if necessary. Turn
into a warmed serving dish and
sprinkle with the remaining
coconut. Serve hot.

Menu Suggestion
This dry curry needs to be
accompanied by vegetables which
are cooked in a sauce. Phool Gobi
Ki Bhaji (Cauliflower in Curry
Sauce) page 92 would be ideal, so
too would Muttar Paneer (Peas
with Cheese) page 91 and Rasedar
Sabzi (Mixed Vegetable Curry)
page 95.

KOFTA KARI
(MEATBALL CURRY)

| 1.15* | 🍳 | ✳ | 446 cals |

MEDIUM
* plus 30 minutes chilling

Serves 4

450 g (1 lb) finely minced beef or
    lamb, or a mixture of the two

2.5 cm (1 inch) piece of fresh root
    ginger, peeled and crushed

2 garlic cloves, skinned and
    crushed

10 ml (2 tsp) garam masala (page
    140)

10 ml (2 tsp) turmeric

5 ml (1 tsp) ground cumin

5 ml (1 tsp) chilli powder

salt

1 egg, beaten

50 ml (2 fl oz) ghee or vegetable oil

1 onion, skinned and chopped

2.5 cm (1 inch) stick cinnamon

6 green cardamoms, crushed

4 cloves

10 ml (2 tsp) paprika

600 ml (1 pint) coconut milk
    (page 134)

vegetable oil, for deep-frying

1 Put the minced meat in a bowl
with half of the ginger, garlic,
garam masala, turmeric, cumin
and chilli powder. Add 5 ml (1 tsp)
salt and mix well with your hands.
Bind with the egg.

2 (If you have a food processor,
put all the ingredients, except
the egg, in the machine and work
for a few seconds. The mixture
will grind to a paste-like

3 With wetted hands, form the
mixture into 24 balls. Chill in
the refrigerator for 30 minutes.

4 Meanwhile, heat the ghee in a
heavy-based saucepan or
flameproof casserole, add the
onion with the remaining ginger
and garlic and fry gently for about
5 minutes until softened.

5 Add the cinnamon,
cardamoms, cloves and
paprika with the remaining garam
masala, turmeric, cumin and chilli
powder. Fry, stirring, for 2
minutes. Pour in 600 ml (1 pint)
water and the coconut milk. Add
salt to taste and bring to the boil.
Simmer until reduced by about
one-third.

6 Heat the oil in a deep-fat fryer
to 190°C (375°F). Add the
meatballs in batches and deep-fry
until golden brown on all sides.
Remove with a slotted spoon and
drain on absorbent kitchen paper.

7 Add the meatballs to the
coconut sauce. Cover and
simmer gently for 30 minutes.
Serve hot.

Menu Suggestion
Meatball Curry can be served for a
family meal, or even for a buffet
party. Khumbi Pullao (Mushroom
Pilau) page 111 makes the perfect
accompaniment.

45

KEEMA MATAR
(SPICED MINCE WITH PEAS)

| 1.15 | £ ✳ | 357–535 cals |

MEDIUM-HOT

Serves 4–6

30 ml (2 tbsp) ghee or vegetable oil

1 medium onion, skinned and finely chopped

2.5 cm (1 inch) piece of fresh root ginger, peeled and grated

8 garlic cloves, skinned and crushed

10 ml (2 tsp) ground cumin

15 ml (1 tbsp) ground coriander

5 ml (1 tsp) chilli powder

2.5 ml ($\frac{1}{2}$ tsp) turmeric

900 g (2 lb) lean minced beef or lamb

226 g (8 oz) can tomatoes, chopped

5 ml (1 tsp) caster sugar

10 ml (2 tsp) salt

350 g (12 oz) frozen peas

45 ml (3 tbsp) chopped fresh coriander, parsley or mint

30 ml (2 tbsp) lemon or lime juice

5 ml (1 tsp) garam masala (page 140), to serve

1 Heat the ghee in a heavy-based saucepan or flameproof casserole, add the onion and cook over high heat until just turning brown. Lower the heat, add the ginger, garlic and spices and cook gently for 2–3 minutes.

2 Add the minced meat, chopped tomatoes and juice, sugar and salt. Stir well until mixed and bring to the boil. Cover and simmer for 45 minutes.

3 Stir in the peas, coriander, parsley and the lemon juice. Cover and simmer for 15 minutes, stirring occasionally.

4 To serve, sprinkle with garam masala. Serve hot.

Menu Suggestion
Serve with Tale Hua Masaledar Aloo (Fried Masala Potatoes) page 85, a dal dish and Parathas page 144.

BHOONA MHAANS
(MARINATED SAUTÉED STEAK)

| 0.30* | £ £ | 408 cals |

MEDIUM

* plus 2 hours marinating

Serves 4

700 g (1½ lb) rump steak

6 green cardamoms

4 cloves

6 black peppercorns

juice of 2 limes

150 ml (¼ pint) natural yogurt

2.5 ml (½ tsp) chilli powder

salt

50 ml (2 fl oz) ghee or vegetable oil

lime slices or wedges, to serve

1 Cut off the fat around the edge of the steak, then cut the meat into serving pieces. Beat with a mallet until flat and thin. Set aside until required.

2 Dry fry the cardamoms, cloves and peppercorns in a heavy-based frying pan, then finely grind in a small electric mill or with a pestle and mortar. Transfer to a bowl and add half of the lime juice, the yogurt, chilli powder and salt to taste. Stir well to mix.

3 Place the pieces of steak on 1–2 plates and brush with half of the marinade. Leave to stand at room temperature for at least 1 hour, then turn the steak pieces over and repeat on the other side.

4 When ready to cook, heat the ghee in a large, heavy-based frying pan until smoking hot. Add the steaks in batches and sear on both sides in the hot fat, then lower the heat and continue frying for about 8 minutes or until cooked to your liking. Turn the steaks frequently during frying.

5 Remove the steaks from the pan and arrange overlapping on a warmed serving dish. Pour the remaining lime juice into the residual fat and stir to combine over high heat. Drizzle the pan juices over the steak and garnish with lime slices or wedges.

Menu Suggestion

Serve for a midweek supper, with Tale Hua Masaledar Aloo (Fried Masala Potatoes) page 85, Piaz Aur Hari Mirch Wali Bhindi (Okra Fried with Onion and Green Chilli) page 88 or Hare Sem Aur Nariyal (Green Beans with Coconut) page 89.

VINDALOO
(HOT SPICY PORK)

| 2.00 | £ | ✳ | 565 cals |

HOT

Serves 4

60 ml (4 tbsp) ghee or vegetable oil

1 large onion, skinned and finely sliced

6–8 whole dried red chillies

10 ml (2 tsp) cumin seeds

10 ml (2 tsp) coriander seeds

10 ml (2 tsp) paprika

10 black peppercorns

2.5 cm (1 inch) stick cinnamon

seeds of 6 green cardamoms

10 ml (2 tsp) mustard seeds

3 whole cloves

2.5 cm (1 inch) piece of fresh root ginger, peeled and chopped

10 garlic cloves, skinned

5 ml (1 tsp) salt

90 ml (6 tbsp) wine vinegar

30 ml (2 tbsp) tomato purée

900 g (2 lb) lean pork shoulder, trimmed of excess fat and cut into 2.5 cm (1 inch) cubes

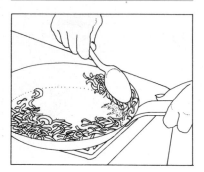

1 Heat half of the ghee in a large, heavy-based pan or flameproof casserole, add the onion and fry over moderate heat until just turning brown.

2 Remove the onion from the casserole with a slotted spoon and place in a blender or food processor.

3 Add the chillies to the machine with the spices, garlic, salt, vinegar, tomato purée and 60 ml (4 tbsp) water. Work until completely smooth.

4 Cut the pork into 2.5 cm (1 inch) cubes and trim off any fat. Heat the remaining ghee in the pan, add the cubes of pork and fry over moderate heat until browned on all sides. Add the onion and spice mixture and cook for a few minutes over high heat, stirring all the time to prevent sticking.

5 Turn down the heat to very low, cover and cook very gently for about 1½ hours or until the meat is tender and the sauce considerably reduced. If the sauce reduces too much before the meat is cooked, add a little extra water. Serve hot.

Menu Suggestion

Vindaloo is an exceptionally hot curry. Serve with Uble Chaval (Plain Boiled Rice) page 109. Raita (Cucumber with Yogurt) page 152 and Aam Ki Chutney (Mango Chutney) page 149 will help cool the palate.

VINDALOO

Vindaloo curries come from Goa in western India. They are always fiery hot. The locally grown red chillies, which are mixed with vinegar, give the vindaloo curry its characteristic hot-sour taste. Traditional vindaloos are made from pork, which the Christians in western India are able to eat, but if you see vindaloo on an Indian restaurant menu it will usually be made with lamb or beef— depending on whether the proprietors of the restaurant are Muslim or Hindu.

SHIKAR KARI
(PORK CURRY)

| 2.00 | ✳ | 555 cals |

MILD-MEDIUM

Serves 4

60 ml (4 tbsp) ghee or vegetable oil

1 medium onion, skinned and finely chopped

2–3 garlic cloves, skinned and crushed

6 green cardamoms

2.5 cm (1 inch) stick cinnamon

4 whole cloves

10 ml (2 tsp) ground ginger

2 fresh green chillies, seeded and finely chopped

900 g (2 lb) boneless pork, trimmed of excess fat and cut into cubes

juice of 1 large lemon

1 large piece of lemon rind

1 large piece of orange rind

5 ml (1 tsp) salt

30 ml (2 tbsp) chopped fresh coriander, to garnish

1 Heat the ghee in a heavy-based saucepan or flameproof casserole, add the onion and garlic and fry gently for about 5 minutes until soft and lightly coloured.

2 Meanwhile, grind the cardamoms, cinnamon and cloves in a small electric mill or with a pestle and mortar.

3 Add the ground spices to the onion mixture with the ginger and chillies. Fry for 2 minutes, stirring constantly.

4 Add the pork to the pan in batches and fry over moderate heat until well browned on all sides. Add the lemon juice and lemon and orange rinds, with the salt. Stir well, add about 300 ml ($\frac{1}{2}$ pint) water to just cover the meat and bring to the boil.

5 Lower the heat, cover and simmer gently, stirring occasionally, for about 1$\frac{1}{2}$ hours or until the pork is tender. Remove the lemon and orange rinds before serving, if preferred, and stir in the coriander. Serve hot.

Menu Suggestion
This pork curry goes well with Peelay Chaval (Yellow Aromatic Rice) page 108 and a dal dish such as Sookhi Moong Dal (Dry Moong Dal) page 100.

DOPIAZA
(PORK CURRY WITH ONIONS)

2.30	✳	616 cals

MILD-MEDIUM

Serves 4

1.1 kg (2½ lb) onions, skinned

100 ml (4 fl oz) ghee or vegetable oil

30 ml (2 tbsp) lime or lemon juice

700 g (1½ lb) boneless pork, trimmed of excess fat and cut into cubes

10 ml (2 tsp) ground coriander

10 ml (2 tsp) turmeric

5 ml (1 tsp) fenugreek seeds

5 ml (1 tsp) salt

2.5–5 ml (½–1 tsp) chilli powder, according to taste

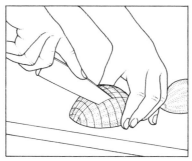

1 Chop half of the onions very finely. Heat the ghee in a heavy-based saucepan or flame-proof casserole, add the onions and the lime or lemon juice and fry very gently for 20 minutes, stirring frequently, until light golden and quite dry. Remove with a slotted spoon and set aside on a plate.

2 Add the pork to the residual ghee in the pan and fry over high heat until well browned on all sides. Transfer with a slotted spoon to a separate plate.

3 Thinly slice the remaining onions. Add to the pan, with the coriander, turmeric, fenugreek, salt and chilli powder. Fry gently for about 10 minutes until the onions are soft, then return the pork to the pan and stir to mix with the onions. Moisten with a little water if necessary, then cover and simmer for 1½ hours or until the pork is tender.

4 Add the reserved chopped onions to the pork and mix well. Continue cooking for about 15 minutes, stirring constantly until the sauce is thick and almost dry. Turn into a warmed serving dish and serve hot.

Menu Suggestion
Serve with one of the Indian breads on pages 142–147, and a vegetable dish such as Hare Sem Aur Nariyal (Green Beans with Coconut) page 89.

KORMA SHEER
(PORK CHOPS WITH ALMOND MILK)

1.30	819 cals

MILD

Serves 4

4 whole cloves

4 green cardamoms

5 ml (1 tsp) black peppercorns

2.5 cm (1 inch) stick cinnamon

75 ml (5 tbsp) ghee or vegetable oil

2 medium onions, skinned and
  thinly sliced

2.5 cm (1 inch) piece of fresh root
  ginger, peeled and crushed

4 pork loin chops, trimmed of
  excess fat

568 ml (1 pint) milk

5 ml (1 tsp) turmeric

salt

50 g (2 oz) blanched almonds

150 ml ($\frac{1}{4}$ pint) double dream

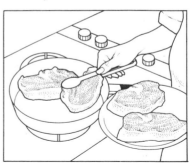

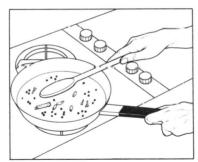

1 Dry fry the cloves,
cardamoms, peppercorns and
cinnamon stick in a large heavy
frying pan for a few minutes, then
grind in a small electric mill or
with a pestle and mortar.

2 Heat 60 ml (4 tbsp) of the ghee
in a flameproof casserole. Add
the onions, ginger and ground
spices and fry gently, stirring
frequently, for about 10 minutes
until softened. Transfer with a
slotted spoon to a jug.

3 Add the remaining ghee to a
large, heavy frying pan, then
the pork chops. Fry until browned
on both sides.

4 Stir the milk into the onion
mixture, then add the turmeric
and 5 ml (1 tsp) salt. Pour over the
chops and bring to the boil. Cover
and simmer for about 45 minutes
until the chops are tender and the
sauce is quite thick and dry. Spoon
the sauce over the chops
occasionally during cooking.

5 Meanwhile, pound the
almonds with a pestle and
mortar, or work in a blender or
food processor. Mix with the
cream in a bowl, then cover and
leave to infuse for 30 minutes.

6 When the chops are tender,
remove from the liquid and
place overlapping on a warmed
serving plate. Cover and keep hot.
Strain the cooking liquid and boil
to reduce, then pour in the almond
cream. Simmer for a further
10 minutes, shaking the pan to
coat the chops evenly in the sauce.

Menu Suggestion
Serve with Sag Aloo (Spinach and
Potatoes) page 86 or Pullao (Fruit
and Nut Pilau) page 112.

GOSHT AUR ALOOCHA
(PORK CHOPS WITH PLUMS)

0.50*	385 cals

MEDIUM-HOT

* plus at least 4 hours or overnight marinating

Serves 4

120 ml (8 tbsp) lime or lemon juice, or a mixture of both

2 garlic cloves, skinned and crushed

10 ml (2 tsp) ground ginger

5 ml (1 tsp) paprika

2.5–5 ml ($\frac{1}{2}$–1 tsp) chilli powder

4 pork loin chops, trimmed of rind and excess fat

570 g (20 oz) can Victoria plums in syrup

salt

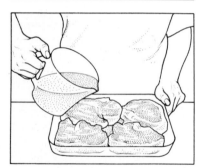

1 Make the marinade. Mix together half of the lime juice, the garlic, ginger, paprika and chilli powder. Put the chops in a single layer in a dish and pour over the marinade. Cover and leave to marinate for at least 4 hours, preferably overnight.

2 When ready to cook, work the plums and syrup through a sieve. (Alternatively, remove the stones and work in a blender or food processor.)

3 Put the plum purée in a heavy-based saucepan with the remaining lime juice and salt to taste. Boil, stirring constantly, until reduced.

4 Brush a little of the plum glaze over 1 side of the chops and place under a preheated moderate grill. Cook for about 5 minutes until glossy, then turn the chops over and brush with more glaze.

5 Continue cooking, turning and glazing the chops for about 20 minutes, until they are cooked to your liking.

Menu Suggestion
Pork Chops with Plums are sweet and spicy. They taste especially good with Phool Gobi Ki Bhaji (Cauliflower in Curry Sauce) page 92 and Uble Chaval (Plain Boiled Rice) page 109.

Chicken and Poultry

Free-range poultry is a
very popular and
inexpensive source of
protein in India. The
tandoori cooking method
suits all kinds of poultry
admirably, and it is used
widely in Indian cookery.
It is also especially
suitable for our modern
battery birds: the
tandoori marinades
improve their bland
flavour and help produce
more succulent flesh.

TIKKA MURGH
(TANDOORI CHICKEN KEBABS)

0.45*	✳*	225 cals

MEDIUM

* plus 24 hours marinating; freeze in
the marinade

Serves 4

4 boneless chicken breasts

150 ml ($\frac{1}{4}$ pint) natural yogurt

2.5 cm (1 inch) piece of fresh root
ginger, peeled and crushed

4 garlic cloves, skinned and
crushed

$\frac{1}{2}$ small onion, skinned and
grated

15 ml (1 tbsp) vinegar

5 ml (1 tsp) chilli powder

2.5 ml ($\frac{1}{2}$ tsp) red or orange food
colouring

5 ml (1 tsp) salt

50 ml (2 fl oz) ghee or melted
butter

lemon wedges, to serve

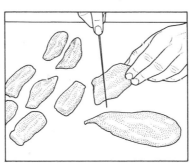

1 Cut the chicken into bite-sized
chunks, removing all skin.
Place in a bowl.

2 Work the yogurt in a blender
or food processor with the
remaining ingredients except the
ghee and lemon wedges.

3 Pour the marinade over the
chicken and stir. Cover and
marinate in the refrigerator for 24
hours.

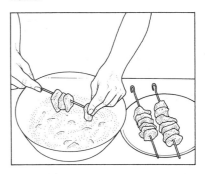

4 Thread the chicken on to
4 oiled skewers. Place on a
barbecue or grill rack and brush
with marinade and ghee.

5 Barbecue or grill the chicken
for about 15 minutes, turning
frequently and brushing with
more marinade and ghee.

Menu Suggestion
Serve with Khumbi Pullao
(Mushroom Pilau) page 111, Sarso
Aur Dahi Me Bhoona Hua Baigan
(Sautéed Aubergines with
Mustard Seeds and Yogurt)
page 94 and Nan (Flat Leavened
White Bread) page 142.

TANDOORI MURGH
(TANDOORI CHICKEN)

1.40* ✳* 315 cals

MEDIUM
* plus 24 hours marinating; freeze in the marinade

Serves 4

4 large chicken portions, each weighing about 10 oz (275 g)

30 ml (2 tbsp) lime or lemon juice

2 garlic cloves, skinned and crushed

5 ml (1 tsp) chilli powder

salt and freshly ground pepper

15 ml (1 tbsp) cumin seeds

15 ml (1 tbsp) coriander seeds

2.5 cm (1 inch) piece of fresh root ginger, peeled and chopped

60 ml (4 tbsp) natural yogurt

10 ml (2 tsp) garam masala (page 140)

2.5 ml (½ tsp) red or orange food colouring

50 ml (2 fl oz) ghee or melted butter

shredded lettuce, onion rings and lemon wedges, to serve

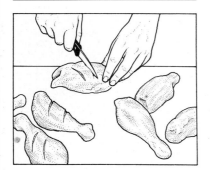

1 Cut each chicken portion in half and remove the skin. Slash each piece of chicken in several places with a sharp, pointed knife.

2 In a bowl, mix together the lime or lemon juice, garlic, chilli powder, 5 ml (1 tsp) salt and plenty of pepper. Rub all over the chicken, then place in a single layer in a shallow dish. Set aside while preparing the remaining ingredients.

3 Grind the cumin and coriander seeds and the ginger in a small electric mill or with a pestle and mortar. Turn into a bowl and mix in the yogurt, garam masala and food colouring.

4 Brush the marinade all over the chicken, working it into the cuts in the flesh. Cover the dish and marinate in the refrigerator for 24 hours.

5 When ready to cook, place the chicken pieces on a rack in a roasting tin. Pour enough water under the rack to just cover the bottom of the tin. Brush the ghee or butter over the chicken, then roast in the oven at 200°C (400°F) mark 6 for 1 hour, turning once and basting with the liquid from the bottom of the tin.

6 To serve, arrange the lettuce and onion rings on a large platter. Place the chicken on top, then garnish with lemon wedges. Serve hot.

Menu Suggestion
Tandoori Chicken is traditionally served with Nan (Flat Leavened White Bread) page 142. Rasedar Sabzi (Mixed Vegetable Curry) page 95 would also make a good accompaniment, with Peelay Chaval (Yellow Aromatic Rice) page 108 if liked.

TANDOORI MURGH
Small tandoori ovens are sold at specialist kitchen shops, but even if you invest in one, it is unlikely that you will achieve the same colour and flavour that come from the traditional clay oven used in Indian restaurants. This recipe works very well in a conventional oven, but if you prefer the chicken pieces to have the charred appearance of authentic tandoori, cook them on a barbecue.

SUFAID MURGH
(CHICKEN COOKED IN COCONUT MILK)

1.15	✳	440 cals

MEDIUM

Serves 4

60 ml (4 tbsp) ghee, sesame or
  vegetable oil

8 chicken pieces, skinned

2 medium onions, skinned and
  roughly chopped

4 garlic cloves, skinned and
  roughly chopped

4–5 cm (1½–2 inch) piece of fresh
  root ginger, peeled and roughly
  chopped

3 dried red chillies

4 whole cloves

2.5 cm (1 inch) stick cinnamon,
  crushed lightly

5 ml (1 tsp) fenugreek seeds,
  dry fried (page 140)

10 ml (2 tsp) coriander seeds,
  dry fried

10 ml (2 tsp) cumin seeds, dry fried

75 ml (5 tbsp) lime or lemon juice

600 ml (1 pint) thin coconut milk
  (page 134)

6 curry leaves, optional

5 ml (1 tsp) salt

15 ml (1 tbsp) sesame seeds, dry
  fried

chopped fresh coriander and lime
  wedges, to garnish

1 Heat the ghee in a deep frying
pan or flameproof casserole,
add the chicken pieces and fry
until golden brown. Remove the
chicken to a plate with a slotted
spoon and set aside.

2 Put the onions in a blender or
food processor with the garlic,
ginger, chillies, cloves, cinnamon,
fenugreek, coriander, cumin and
lime juice. Work until smooth,
adding a little water if necessary.

3 Add this mixture to the frying
pan. Fry gently, stirring all the
time, for 5 minutes until the paste
turns a golden brown.

4 Add the coconut milk, the
curry leaves and salt. Stir well,
then return the chicken pieces to
the frying pan.

5 Bring to the boil, then lower
the heat, cover and simmer for
about 50 minutes or until the
chicken is tender and the sauce
slightly thickened.

6 Transfer the chicken and
sauce to a warmed serving dish
and sprinkle with the sesame seeds
and chopped coriander. Garnish
with the lime wedges and serve
immediately.

Menu Suggestion
Serve for a dinner party main
course, with Masaledal Basmati
(Spiced Fried Basmati Rice)
page 107 and Chapatis
(Unleavened Wholemeal Bread)
page 144. Piaz Aur Hari Mirch
Wali Bhindi (Okra Fried with
Onion and Green Chilli) page 88
would make a suitable vegetable
accompaniment.

KORMA MURGH
(CHICKEN WITH CASHEWS, SPICES AND YOGURT)

| 1.25 | 🍳 | £ £ | 485 cals |

MILD

Serves 4

50 g (2 oz) unsalted cashew nuts or
    blanched almonds

2 garlic cloves, skinned and
    roughly chopped

2.5 cm (1 inch) piece of fresh root
    ginger, peeled and roughly
    chopped

5 cm (2 inch) stick cinnamon,
    lightly crushed

2 whole cloves

seeds of 4 green cardamoms

50 g (2 oz) white poppy seeds

10 ml (2 tsp) coriander seeds

5 ml (1 tsp) cumin seeds

5 ml (1 tsp) chilli powder

5 ml (1 tsp) salt

5 ml (1 tsp) saffron threads

45 ml (3 tbsp) ghee or vegetable
    oil

2 medium onions, skinned and
    finely chopped

150 ml ($\frac{1}{4}$ pint) natural yogurt

8 chicken pieces, skinned

30 ml (2 tbsp) chopped fresh
    coriander or parsley

30 ml (2 tbsp) chopped fresh mint
    or 10 ml (2 tsp) dried

45 ml (3 tbsp) lemon juice

sprigs of fresh mint or coriander,
    to garnish

1 Put the cashew nuts, garlic, ginger and 150 ml ($\frac{1}{4}$ pint) water into a blender or food processor and work until smooth.

2 Grind the cinnamon, cloves, cardamom, poppy, coriander and cumin seeds in a small electric mill or with a pestle and mortar until a fine powder.

3 Add the ground spices to the nut mixture with the chilli powder and salt. Set aside.

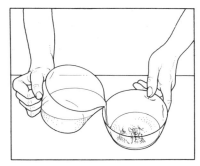

4 Place the saffron threads in a bowl, pour over 300 ml ($\frac{1}{2}$ pint) boiling water and leave to soak for 15 minutes.

5 Heat the ghee in a deep frying pan or flameproof casserole, add the chopped onion and fry gently for 10 minutes, stirring occasionally, until softened and golden brown.

6 Add the spice and nut mixture and the yogurt and continue cooking, stirring all the time, until the ghee begins to separate.

7 Add the saffron water with the saffron threads and stir well. Add the chicken pieces and bring to the boil, then lower the heat, cover and simmer gently for 45 minutes, stirring occasionally.

8 Add the chopped coriander and mint. Sprinkle over the lemon juice. Cover the pan again and cook for a further 15 minutes or until the chicken is tender and the sauce thickened.

9 Transfer the chicken and sauce to a warmed serving dish and garnish with the mint or coriander sprigs. Serve hot.

Menu Suggestion
This is a very special chicken dish. Serve for a dinner party main course with Chapatis (Unleavened Wholemeal Bread) page 144 and Masaledal Basmati (Spiced Fried Basmati Rice) page 107. A suitable vegetable accompaniment would be Hare Sem Aur Nariyal (Green Beans with Coconut) page 89.

MURGH BHOONA
(MARINATED STIR-FRIED CHICKEN)

| 0.30* | £ | 345 cals |

MILD

* plus at least 2 hours marinating

Serves 4

4 large boneless chicken breasts

90 ml (6 tbsp) natural yogurt

juice of 1 lime or lemon juice

2 garlic cloves, skinned and crushed

2.5 ml ($\frac{1}{2}$ tsp) turmeric

15 ml (1 tbsp) paprika

seeds of 3 green cardamoms, crushed

2.5 ml ($\frac{1}{2}$ tsp) salt

60 ml (4 tbsp) ghee or vegetable oil

2.5 ml ($\frac{1}{2}$ tsp) garam masala (page 140)

30 ml (2 tbsp) chopped fresh coriander

lime or lemon wedges, to garnish

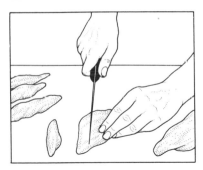

1 Skin the chicken breasts and cut the flesh into strips about 1 cm ($\frac{1}{2}$ inch) wide. Put the strips into a bowl with the yogurt, lime juice, garlic, turmeric, paprika, cardamom seeds and salt. Mix well to coat.

2 Melt 30 ml (2 tbsp) ghee in a small saucepan. Stir into the chicken mixture, cover and leave to marinate in the refrigerator for at least 2 hours.

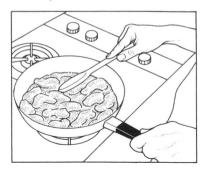

3 Heat the remaining ghee in a heavy frying pan or wok. Add the chicken and marinade and stir-fry for 10 minutes.

4 Lower the heat and add the garam masala and coriander. Stir-fry for a further 5–10 minutes until the chicken is tender. Transfer to a warmed serving dish, garnish with lime wedges and serve immediately.

Menu Suggestion
This stir-fried dish is quick and easy to make, ideal for a family midweek supper. Serve with Uble Chaval (Plain Boiled Rice) page 109 and a pulse dish such as Masoor Ki Dal, Baigan Aur Khumbi (Masoor Dal with Aubergine and Mushrooms) page 98, if you have the time.

MURGH BHOONA

The technique of stir-frying in this quick chicken dish is correctly called sukha bhoona. The chicken is very quickly stir-fried or sautéed in a small amount of ghee until tender. It is quite a skill to achieve the right consistency with this cooking method, which can only really come with practice. Choose a heavy-based frying pan, preferably cast iron, and take care not to have the heat too fierce.

MURGH MASALLAM
(WHOLE CHICKEN COOKED WITH YOGURT AND SPICES)

 1.30* | 390 cals

MILD

* plus 2 hours marinating

Serves 4

1.4 kg (3 lb) chicken
60 ml (4 tbsp) lemon or lime juice
2 garlic cloves, skinned and finely chopped
2.5 cm (1 inch) piece of fresh root ginger, peeled and finely chopped
10 ml (2 tsp) ground cumin
10 ml (2 tsp) ground coriander
5 ml (1 tsp) garam masala (page 140)
10 ml (2 tsp) salt
2.5 ml (½ tsp) freshly ground pepper
45 ml (3 tbsp) ghee or vegetable oil
2 medium onions, skinned and finely sliced
5 ml (1 tsp) turmeric
2.5 ml (½ tsp) cayenne
300 ml (½ pint) natural yogurt
50 g (2 oz) unsalted cashew nuts or blanched almonds
chopped fresh coriander, to garnish

2 Mix the lemon juice with the garlic, ginger, cumin, coriander, garam masala, salt and pepper. Rub all over the chicken, working the mixture into the incisions. Cover and leave to marinate in the refrigerator for about 2 hours.

3 Heat the ghee in a frying pan, add the onions and fry gently for 8–10 minutes until soft and golden brown. Add the tumeric and cayenne and fry for a further 2 minutes.

4 Add the yogurt, 15 ml (1 tbsp) at a time. Cook each addition over high heat, stirring constantly, until the yogurt is absorbed.

5 Transfer the onion and yogurt mixture to a blender or food processor. Add the cashew nuts and work until smooth.

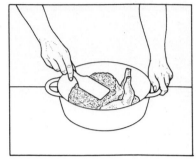

6 Place the chicken in a casserole or roasting tin and spread the onion mixture all over the bird. Cover with a lid or foil, then bake in the oven at 180°C (350°F) mark 4, basting frequently, for about 1 hour or until the chicken is tender.

7 Transfer the chicken to a warmed serving dish and spoon over the sauce. Sprinkle with the chopped coriander and serve immediately.

Menu Suggestion
Serve this whole roast chicken as an unusual alternative to a traditional roast. Nan (Flat Leavened White Bread) page 142, Rasedar Sabzi (Mixed Vegetable Curry) page 95 and Masaledal Basmati (Spiced Fried Basmati Rice) page 107 make ideal accompaniments.

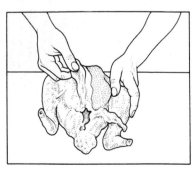

1 Skin the chicken completely, leaving it whole. With a sharp knife, make small incisions all over the bird. Place in a large bowl.

MURGH MASALLAM

This roast chicken is a very special dish in India, often served at feasts and other celebration meals and called "royal" or "regal" chicken. The chicken is cooked by the *dum bhoona* method; that is it is tightly covered and pot roasted in the oven so that all the flavour and juices of the bird are sealed in. In India, Murgh Masallam is traditionally cooked in a pot over charcoal with extra charcoal placed on top of the lid. A good method of cooking Murgh Masallam at home is to wrap it completely in a tight foil parcel, then place it in a roasting tin in case any juices escape.

CHIRGA
(SPICED ROAST CHICKEN)

| 2.45 | 550 cals |

MILD

Serves 4

1.8 kg (4 lb) oven-ready chicken

juice of 1 lemon

10 ml (2 tsp) coriander seeds, finely crushed

2.5 ml ($\frac{1}{2}$ tsp) chilli powder

300 ml ($\frac{1}{2}$ pint) natural yogurt

60 ml (4 tbsp) chopped fresh coriander

60 ml (4 tbsp) chopped fresh mint

5 cm (2 inch) piece of fresh root ginger, peeled and crushed

4 garlic cloves, skinned and crushed

5 ml (1 tsp) paprika

5 ml (1 tsp) turmeric

5 ml (1 tsp) salt

50 ml (2 fl oz) ghee or melted butter

coriander and mint sprigs and lemon wedges, to garnish

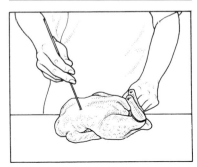

1 Prick the skin of the chicken all over with a fine skewer. Mix together the lemon juice, crushed coriander seeds and the chilli powder and brush over the chicken. Leave for 30 minutes.

2 Meanwhile, mix together the remaining ingredients, except the ghee and the garnish.

3 Stand the chicken, breast side up, in a roasting tin. Brush with one-quarter of the yogurt mixture. Roast in the oven at 200°C (400°F) mark 6 for about 30 minutes or until the yogurt dries.

4 Turn the chicken over on its side and brush with another quarter of the yogurt mixture. Return to the oven for a further 30 minutes until the yogurt dries again. Continue turning the chicken and brushing with yogurt twice more, until the chicken has been cooking for 2 hours.

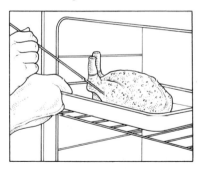

5 Stand the chicken, breast side up again, and brush with the ghee. Increase the oven temperature to 220°C (425°F) mark 7 and roast the chicken for a further 15 minutes or until the juices run clear when the thickest part of a thigh is pierced with a skewer.

6 Transfer the chicken to a warmed dish. Garnish and serve immediately.

Menu Suggestion

Chirga is spicy but dry. Serve with a juicy vegetable dish such as Phool Gobi Ki Bhaji (Cauliflower in Curry Sauce) page 92 or Muttar Paneer (Peas with Cheese) page 91.

VATH
(ROAST DUCK WITH CASHEW NUT STUFFING)

3.00	🥢	£ £	715 cals

MILD

Serves 4

2.3–2.7 kg (5–6 lb) duck
45 ml (3 tbsp) ghee or vegetable oil
1 onion, skinned and finely chopped
2 garlic cloves, skinned and crushed
10 ml (2 tsp) ground cumin
seeds of 6 green cardamoms, crushed
2.5 ml ($\frac{1}{2}$ tsp) turmeric
100 g (4 oz) fresh white breadcrumbs
75 g (3 oz) unsalted cashew nuts
50 g (2 oz) seedless raisins
30 ml (2 tbsp) chopped fresh coriander
salt and freshly ground pepper
1 egg, beaten

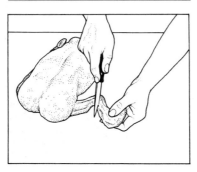

1 First bone the duck. Place the bird breast side up on a board. Cut off the wings at the second joint, the legs at the first.

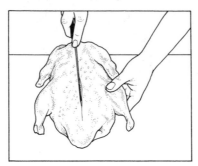

2 Turn the bird breast side down. Cut cleanly through the skin and flesh down the centre of the back from vent to neck.

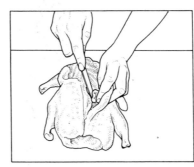

3 Keeping the knife close to the carcass and slightly flattened, carefully work the flesh off the rib cage on one side until the wing joint is exposed; sever the joint. Repeat on the other side.

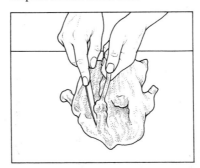

4 Continue working the flesh off the carcass until the leg joint is exposed. Sever the ligaments attaching the bone to the body flesh and break the leg joint by twisting it firmly. Repeat on the other side.

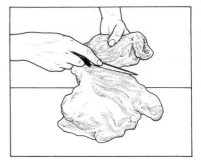

5 Continue working the flesh off the rest of the main frame. Take care not to cut the skin over the breast bone, where the flesh becomes very thin, as the 2 halves of the breast must remain attached to each other.

6 Cut away all visible surplus fat from the duck, then wash the duck under cold running water and pat dry with absorbent kitchen paper. Lay the bird out flat on a clean board, skin side downwards.

7 Make the stuffing. Heat the ghee in a heavy-based frying pan, add the onion and garlic and fry gently for 5 minutes until soft and lightly coloured. Add the spices and fry, stirring, for a further 2 minutes, then turn the mixture into a bowl.

8 Add the breadcrumbs to the onion mixture with the cashew nuts, raisins, coriander and salt and pepper to taste. Mix well, then bind with the beaten egg.

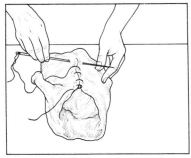

9 Put the stuffing in the centre of the duck, then bring up the side of the bird to enclose the stuffing. Sew with trussing string along where the skin was cut.

10 Turn the duck the right way up and tuck under the neck and end flaps. Sew them to make a neat 'parcel' shape.

11 Truss the bird to hold the wings and legs close to the body. Weigh the stuffed duck and calculate the cooking time, allowing 30–35 minutes per 450 g (1 lb). Put the duck on a wire rack in a roasting tin. Prick the skin of the duck all over to let the fat escape and sprinkle the breast with salt and pepper. Roast in the oven at 180°C (350°F) mark 4 for the calculated cooking time. Serve hot, carved into neat slices.

Menu Suggestion
This roast duck makes an excellent main course for a special dinner or lunch party. Serve Khumbi Pullao (Mushroom Pilau) page 111 or Peelay Chaval (Yellow Aromatic Rice) page 108 as a side dish, with a pulse and vegetable dish such as Chhole (Chick Peas Stewed with Tomatoes) page 103.

Fish and Shellfish

The recipes in this chapter have been adapted from traditional Indian fish recipes to suit varieties of fish which are commonly available in the West. India is a vast country with numerous rivers; it is also surrounded by sea on three sides, therefore there are literally countless different species of fish to be found—many of which are purely local to a tiny area.

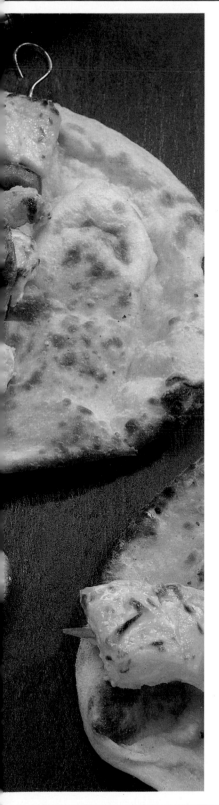

KABAB TIKKAH MACHCHLI
(FISH KEBABS)

0.40*	230 cals

MEDIUM

* plus 4 hours marinating

Serves 4

60 ml (4 tbsp) natural yogurt

2 green chillies, seeded and roughly chopped

2.5 cm (1 inch) piece of fresh root ginger, peeled and chopped

1 garlic clove, skinned and chopped

10 ml (2 tsp) cumin seeds

5 ml (1 tsp) black peppercorns

2.5 ml ($\frac{1}{2}$ tsp) turmeric

2.5 ml ($\frac{1}{2}$ tsp) salt

700 g (1$\frac{1}{2}$ lb) thick white fish fillets (eg monkfish, halibut, turbot, hake, haddock or cod)

12 large prawns, peeled

1 large green pepper

50 ml (2 fl oz) ghee or melted butter

1 First make the marinade. Put the yogurt in a blender or food processor with the chillies, ginger, garlic, cumin seeds, peppercorns, turmeric and salt. Work to a paste. (Alternatively, grind the chillies, ginger, garlic, cumin seeds and peppercorns in a small electric mill or with a pestle and mortar, then stir in the yogurt, turmeric and salt.) Turn into a bowl.

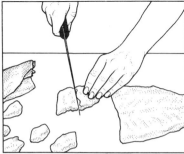

2 Cut the white fish into 16 large chunks, discarding the skin and any bones. Place in the marinade, together with the prawns. Cover and marinate in the refrigerator for 4 hours.

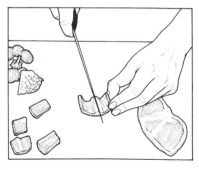

3 Meanwhile, cut the green pepper in half and remove the core and seeds. Cut the flesh into 12 neat squares.

4 When ready to cook, thread the ingredients on to 4 oiled flat kebab skewers, allowing 4 pieces of white fish, 3 pieces of green pepper and 3 prawns on each skewer.

5 Barbecue or grill the kebabs for about 15 minutes or until the fish is cooked, brushing frequently with the ghee or melted butter. Serve hot, with lime or lemon wedges.

Menu Suggestion
Serve these spicy fish kebabs for a starter or a light main course, with Nan (Flat Leavened White Bread) page 142 and Raita (Cucumber with Yogurt) page 152.

TALI MACHCHLI
(SPICED GRILLED MACKEREL)

| 0.40* 🍴 £ | 470 cals |

MEDIUM

* plus 2 hours marinating

Serves 4

4 fresh mackerel, each weighing about 275 g (10 oz), gutted and cleaned

juice of 1 lemon

60 ml (4 tbsp) chopped fresh coriander

10 ml (2 tsp) garam masala (page 140)

5 ml (1 tsp) ground cumin

5 ml (1 tsp) chilli powder

salt and freshly ground pepper

50 ml (2 fl oz) ghee or melted butter

lemon wedges, to serve

1 First bone the mackerel. With a sharp knife, cut off the heads just behind the gills. Extend the cut along the belly to both ends of the fish so that the fish can be opened out.

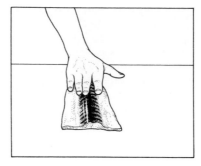

2 Place the fish flat on a board, skin side facing upwards. With the heel of your hand, press along the backbone to loosen it.

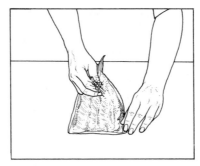

3 Turn the fish right way up and lift out the backbone, using the tip of the knife if necessary to help pull the bone away from the flesh cleanly. Discard the bone.

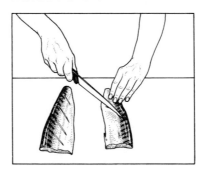

4 Remove the tail and cut each fish in half lengthways, then wash under cold running water and pat dry with absorbent kitchen paper. Score the skin side in several places with a knife.

5 In a jug, mix together the lemon juice, half of the coriander, the garam masala, cumin, chilli powder and salt and pepper to taste.

6 Put the mackerel in a grill pan and pour over the marinade. Cover and leave at cool room temperature for 2 hours, turning the fish once and brushing with the marinade.

7 When ready to cook, brush half of the ghee over the skin side of the mackerel. Cook under a preheated moderate grill for 5 minutes, then turn the fish over and brush with the remaining ghee. Grill for a further 5 minutes.

8 Transfer the fish to a warmed platter and sprinkle with the remaining coriander. Serve immediately, accompanied by lemon wedges.

Menu Suggestion

Spiced Grilled Mackerel is an economical dish for a midweek family meal. Serve with Tale Hua Masaledar Aloo (Fried Masala Potatoes) page 85 or Sag Aloo (Spinach and Potatoes) page 86.

TALI MACHCHLI

The spicy lemon marinade used in this recipe goes especially well with oily fish such as mackerel. In India there are numerous different varieties of both fresh- and sea-water fish, none of which are available here. The marinade can be used instead for familiar fish: fillets of plaice, haddock or cod, or even cubes of thick white monkfish, turbot or hake make excellent kebabs, especially when cooked outside on the barbecue.

SARSO WALI MACHCHLI
(MONKFISH WITH MUSTARD SEEDS)

| 0.35* | £ | 265 cals |

MILD
* plus several hours soaking

Serves 6

45 ml (3 tbsp) black mustard seeds

900 g (2 lb) monkfish fillet, skinned

30 ml (2 tbsp) plain flour

60 ml (4 tbsp) mustard oil or
    vegetable oil

1 medium onion, skinned and
    thinly sliced

300 ml ($\frac{1}{2}$ pint) natural yogurt

1 garlic clove, skinned and
    crushed

15 ml (1 tbsp) lemon juice

salt and freshly ground pepper

whole prawns and coriander,
    to garnish

1 Place 30 ml (2 tbsp) of the mustard seeds in a small bowl. Cover with 60 ml (4 tbsp) water and leave to soak for several hours. Finely grind the remaining seeds in a small electric mill or with a pestle and mortar.

2 Cut the monkfish into 2.5 cm (1 inch) cubes and toss in the flour and ground mustard seeds.

3 Heat the oil in a large heavy-based frying pan, add the onion and fry for about 5 minutes until golden.

4 Drain the mustard seeds, then add to the pan with the monkfish. Fry over moderate heat for 3–4 minutes, turning *very gently* once or twice.

5 Gradually stir in the yogurt with the garlic, lemon juice and salt and pepper to taste. Bring to the boil, then lower the heat and simmer for 10–15 minutes or until the fish is almost tender.

6 Taste and adjust the seasoning. Turn into a warmed serving dish and garnish with the prawns and coriander. Serve immediately.

Menu Suggestion
Serve as a main course, with Pappar (Poppadoms) page 18 and Peelay Chaval (Yellow Aromatic Rice) page 108.

SARSO WALI MACHCHLI
Mustard seeds, called sarson or rai, come in three different colours: black, brown and white. The black seeds are said to be the best, and are the ones most frequently used in Indian cooking. If you have difficulty finding them, go to an Indian or Pakistani grocer and he will be sure to stock them. To obtain their full flavour, it is a good idea to dry roast them before grinding.

MACHCHLI JOUR
(FISH IN SPICY SAUCE WITH TOMATOES)

| 0.35 | £ | 275 cals |

MEDIUM

Serves 4

700 g (1½ lb) white fish such as cod, halibut or haddock, skinned and filleted

60 ml (4 tbsp) ghee or vegetable oil

7.5 ml (1½ tsp) coriander seeds

5 ml (1 tsp) black peppercorns

1 garlic clove, skinned and crushed

5 ml (1 tsp) turmeric

1.25 ml (¼ tsp) chilli powder

5 ml (1 tsp) salt

4 tomatoes, skinned and roughly chopped

2.5 ml (½ tsp) garam masala (page 140)

chopped fresh coriander, to garnish

1 Wash the fish under cold running water and pat dry with absorbent kitchen paper. Cut into 2.5 cm (1 inch) cubes.

2 Heat the ghee in a heavy-based frying pan. Add the fish a few pieces at a time and fry gently for 2–3 minutes.

3 Remove the fish carefully from the pan with a slotted spoon and set aside on a plate.

4 Grind the coriander seeds, peppercorns and garlic in a small electric mill or with a pestle and mortar to a smooth paste.

5 Add the spice paste to the frying pan with the turmeric, chilli powder and salt, and fry gently for 2 minutes.

6 Stir in the tomatoes and 300 ml (½ pint) water. Bring to the boil, then lower the heat and cook over a medium heat for 5 minutes. Add the fish and simmer, shaking the pan occasionally, for a further 10 minutes or until the fish is tender. DO NOT STIR. Remove from the heat.

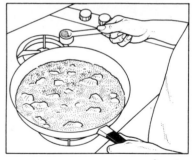

7 Sprinkle the garam masala over the fish, cover the pan and let the fish stand for 2 minutes, then turn into a warmed serving dish. Garnish with the chopped fresh coriander and serve immediately.

Menu Suggestion

This spiced fish dish makes an excellent family supper dish as it is so quick and easy to make. Serve with simple accompaniments such as Uble Chaval (Plain Boiled Rice) page 109 or Khumbi Pullao (Mushroom Pilau) page 111 and Raita (Cucumber with Yogurt) page 152.

MACHCHLI KARI
(WHITE FISH CURRY)

1.20	496 cals

MEDIUM

Serves 4

900 g (2 lb) thick cod steaks or cod fillet, skinned and cut into large cubes

45 ml (3 tbsp) plain flour

75 ml (3 fl oz) ghee or vegetable oil

1 medium onion, skinned and finely chopped

1 cm ($\frac{1}{2}$ inch) piece of fresh root ginger, peeled and very finely chopped or crushed

1–2 garlic cloves, skinned and crushed

2 green chillies, seeded and finely chopped

10 ml (2 tsp) turmeric

10 ml (2 tsp) ground coriander

4 ripe tomatoes, skinned and roughly chopped

salt and freshly ground pepper

50 g (2 oz) creamed coconut

15 ml (1 tbsp) lime or lemon juice

15 ml (1 tbsp) chopped fresh coriander

1 Coat the cubes of fish in the flour. Heat 50 ml (2 fl oz) ghee in a heavy-based frying-pan or flameproof casserole, add the fish and fry for a few minutes over moderate heat until lightly coloured on all sides. Remove with a slotted spoon and set aside.

2 Add the remaining ghee and the onion to the pan with the ginger, garlic and chillies. Fry gently for about 10 minutes, stirring frequently until softened.

3 Add the turmeric and coriander and fry for a further 2 minutes, then add the tomatoes and salt and pepper to taste. Simmer while preparing the coconut milk.

4 Grate or finely chop the creamed coconut into a jug. Slowly pour in 300 ml ($\frac{1}{2}$ pint) boiling water, stirring all the time until the coconut has dissolved.

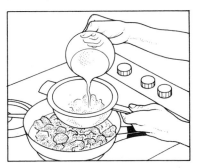

5 Strain the coconut milk into the pan, then bring slowly to boiling point, stirring. Lower the heat, add the fish and fold gently to mix.

6 Cover the frying-pan and simmer gently for 10–15 minutes until the fish is tender. Do not stir throughout the cooking time or the fish will break up; shake the pan gently from time to time.

7 Gently stir in the lime or lemon juice and the coriander. Taste and adjust seasoning, then pour over the fish. Serve immediately.

Menu Suggestion
Serve this fish curry with Sag Aloo (Spinach and Potatoes) page 86 or Peelay Chaval (Yellow Aromatic Rice) page 108.

MACHCHLI KARI

White fish simmered in a thick, spicy coconut sauce is an unusual Indian curry, although the Malaysians and Indonesians frequently cook fish in this way. One of the problems with using white fish is that its delicate flesh tends to break up and flake. One easy way to avoid this is to use frozen fish. Skin the fish while it is still solid, cut it into cubes, then coat in flour and continue with the recipe as for fresh fish.

RASEDAR JHINGA
(PRAWNS IN COCONUT MILK)

| 0.30 | £ £ | 200 cals |

MEDIUM

Serves 4

700 g (1½ lb) medium raw prawns
in the shell or 900 g (2 lb) large
frozen cooked prawns, thawed

10 ml (2 tsp) wine vinegar

5 ml (1 tsp) salt

2.5 cm (1 inch) piece of fresh root
ginger, peeled and finely
chopped

2 garlic cloves, skinned and
crushed

2 medium onions, skinned and
roughly chopped

45 ml (3 tbsp) ghee or vegetable oil

15 ml (1 tbsp) coriander seeds

10 ml (2 tsp) cumin seeds

5 ml (1 tsp) turmeric

2.5 ml (½ tsp) chilli powder

300 ml (½ pint) thick coconut milk
(page 134)

chopped fresh coriander and
sliced and seeded green chillies,
to garnish

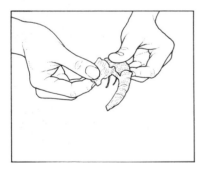

1 If using the raw prawns,
remove the shells with your
fingers leaving on the tail.

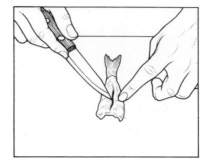

2 With the point of a sharp
knife, cut down the back of
each prawn and remove and
discard the dark vein.

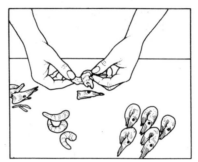

3 If using cooked prawns,
remove the *whole* shell and
de-vein in the same way as the raw
prawns.

4 Wash the prawns and pat dry
with absorbent kitchen paper.
Place in a bowl with the vinegar
and salt and leave to marinate for
30 minutes.

5 Place the ginger, garlic and
onions in a blender or food
processor and work to a smooth
paste, adding a little water if the
mixture sticks. Set aside.

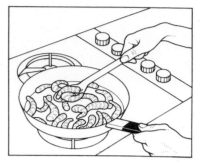

6 Heat half of the ghee in a
heavy-based frying pan and
add the prawns, reserving the
marinade. Toss the raw prawns in
the pan for 3–5 minutes until just
turning pink. If using cooked
prawns, toss for 1–2 minutes only.
Remove the prawns with a slotted
spoon, put back into the marinade
and set aside.

7 Heat the remaining ghee in the
same pan and add the onion
paste. Fry gently for 5 minutes
until just turning golden brown.
Stir in the coriander, cumin,
turmeric and chilli powder and
fry, stirring constantly, for
1 minute.

8 Add the prawns and marinade
and stir well to coat, then pour
in the coconut milk and mix well.
Bring to the boil, then lower the
heat and simmer for 5 minutes.

9 Turn into a warmed serving
dish and garnish with the
chopped fresh coriander and rings
of green chilli. Serve immediately.

Menu Suggestion
Serve for a quick supper or lunch
dish, with Uble Chaval (Plain
Boiled Rice) page 109 and
Pudeene Ki Chutney (Mint
Chutney) page 149.

SAAG JHINGA
(PRAWNS WITH SPINACH)

| 0.35 | £ £ ✳* | 373 cals |

MEDIUM

Serves 4

60 ml (4 tbsp) ghee or vegetable oil

1 small onion, skinned and finely
   chopped

10 ml (2 tsp) ground ginger

10 ml (2 tsp) garam masala
   (page 140)

5 ml (1 tsp) mustard seeds

2.5 ml ($\frac{1}{2}$ tsp) chilli powder

2.5 ml ($\frac{1}{2}$ tsp) turmeric

450 g (1 lb) peeled prawns, thawed
   and thoroughly dried if frozen

450 g (1 lb) frozen leaf spinach

60 ml (4 tbsp) desiccated coconut

5 ml (1 tsp) salt

1 Heat half of the ghee in a heavy-based saucepan or flameproof casserole, add the onion and fry gently for about 5 minutes until soft.

2 Add the spices and fry, stirring, for a further 2 minutes. Add the prawns, increase the heat and toss to coat in the spiced onion mixture. Remove with a slotted spoon and set aside.

3 Heat the remaining ghee in the pan, add the spinach and heat gently until thawed. Stir frequently and cook for 8–10 minutes, or according to packet instructions.

4 Return the prawns to the pan, add half of the coconut and the salt and fold gently to mix. Cook for 5 minutes to allow the flavours to mingle, then turn into a warmed serving dish. Sprinkle with the remaining coconut and serve immediately.

Menu Suggestion

These prawns taste absolutely delicious served with Uble Chaval (Plain Boiled Rice) page 109, crisp Pappar (Poppadoms) page 18 and Raita (Cucumber with Yogurt) page 152.

JHINGA TANDOORI
(TANDOORI PRAWNS)

0.30* £ £ | 165 cals

MILD-MEDIUM
* plus 4 hours marinating
Serves 2

60 ml (4 tbsp) natural yogurt

2.5 cm (1 inch) piece of fresh root ginger, peeled and chopped

1 large garlic clove, skinned and roughly chopped

30 ml (2 tbsp) lime or lemon juice

10 ml (2 tsp) ground cumin

5 ml (1 tsp) garam masala (page 140)

5 ml (1 tsp) salt

seeds of 6 green cardamoms

1.25 ml ($\frac{1}{4}$ tsp) cayenne

10 ml (2 tsp) yellow food colouring

5 ml (1 tsp) red food colouring

8 'jumbo' Mediterranean prawns, in their shells

30 ml (2 tbsp) ghee or melted butter

1 First make the marinade. Put the yogurt in a blender or food processor with the ginger, garlic, lime or lemon juice, cumin, garam masala, salt, cardamoms and cayenne. Work to a paste, then turn into a bowl and stir in the food colouring. (Alternatively, crush the ginger and garlic with a pestle and mortar, then turn into a bowl and stir in the yogurt and lime or lemon juice with the spices, salt and food colouring.)

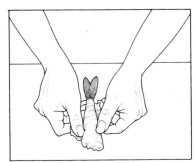

2 Loosen the shell underneath the prawns, then score the exposed flesh with a fork.

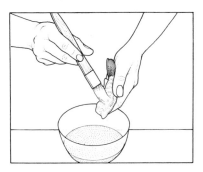

3 Brush the prawns with the marinade, working it under the shells and into the scored flesh as much as possible. Place in a shallow dish or on a plate, cover and marinate in the refrigerator for about 4 hours.

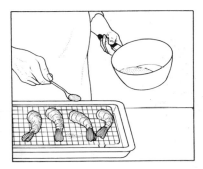

4 When ready to cook, place the prawns on an oiled barbecue grid or grill rack. Sprinkle with some of the ghee.

5 Cook the prawns over or under moderate heat for about 10 minutes. Turn the prawns once during cooking and sprinkle with the remaining ghee. Serve hot.

Menu Suggestion
These prawns make a fabulous dinner party starter. Serve them with Nan (Flat Leavened White Bread) page 142, or Pappar (Poppadoms) page 18 and Champagne or a sparkling dry white wine.

Vegetable and Vegetarian Dishes

A large part of the population of India — particularly in the south — is vegetarian, and Indian vegetable dishes must be amongst the best in the world. In this chapter you will find a good cross-section of the many imaginative ways in which Indians cook vegetables, from everyday potatoes, cauliflower and peas, to the more unusual pulses or dal.

TALE HUA MASALEDAR ALOO
(FRIED MASALA POTATOES)

| 0.35 | 346–518 cals |

MEDIUM

Serves 4–6

900 g (2 lb) new potatoes

ghee or vegetable oil, for
   deep-frying

10 ml (2 tsp) cumin seeds

15 ml (1 tbsp) coriander seeds

7.5 ml (1½ tsp) garam masala
   (page 140)

2.5 cm (1 inch) piece of fresh root
   ginger, peeled and roughly
   chopped

4 garlic cloves, skinned

2 medium onions, skinned and
   chopped

45 ml (3 tbsp) ghee or vegetable oil

5 ml (1 tsp) chilli powder

2.5 ml (½ tsp) turmeric

5 ml (1 tsp) salt

300 ml (½ pint) natural yogurt

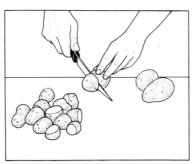

1 Wash the potatoes and scrub
clean if necessary. Cut into
2.5 cm (1 inch) pieces. Pat dry
with absorbent kitchen paper.

2 Heat the oil in a deep-fat fryer
to 180°C (350°F) and deep-fry
the potatoes in batches for 10
minutes or until golden brown.
Remove from the oil and drain on
absorbent kitchen paper.

3 Place the cumin and coriander
seeds in a blender or food
processor with the garam masala,
ginger, garlic and onions. Work
until smooth, adding a little water
if necessary.

4 Heat the ghee in a heavy-based
frying pan, add the masala
paste and fry gently for about 5
minutes. Add the chilli, turmeric
and salt and fry for a further 1
minute.

5 Pour in the yogurt, then add
the potatoes. Stir well and
cook for another 5 minutes until
completely heated through. Serve
piping hot.

Menu Suggestion

Fried Masala Potatoes are a
versatile vegetable dish. They can
be served with most Indian meat
and fish dishes, or with other
vegetables such as Sarso Aur Dahi
Me Bhoona Hua Baigan (Sautéed
Aubergines with Mustard Seeds
and Yogurt) page 94 and Puris
(Deep-fried Unleavened
Wholemeal Bread) page 142 to
make a substantial and varied
vegetarian meal.

SAG ALOO
(SPINACH AND POTATOES)

| 0.40 | £ | ✳ | 193–290 cals |

MILD

Serves 4–6

900 g (2 lb) fresh spinach, or 450 g (1 lb) frozen leaf spinach, thawed and drained

60 ml (4 tbsp) ghee or vegetable oil

1 medium onion, skinned and thinly sliced

2 garlic cloves, skinned and crushed

10 ml (2 tsp) ground coriander

5 ml (1 tsp) black mustard seeds

2.5 ml ($\frac{1}{2}$ tsp) turmeric

1.25 ml ($\frac{1}{4}$ tsp) chilli powder

1.25 ml ($\frac{1}{4}$ tsp) ground ginger

salt

450 g (1 lb) old potatoes, peeled and thickly sliced

1 If using fresh spinach, wash well, put in a large saucepan without any water and cook over very gentle heat for about 15 minutes. Drain well. Cool.

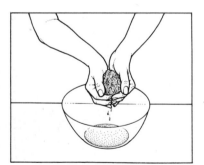

2 With your hands, squeeze out all the moisture from the spinach. Place on a board and chop finely.

3 (If using frozen spinach, cook over very gentle heat for about 5 minutes to drive off as much liquid as possible.)

4 Melt the ghee in a heavy-based saucepan or flameproof casserole, add the onion, garlic, spices and salt to taste and fry gently for about 5 minutes, stirring frequently, until the onion begins to brown.

5 Add the potatoes and stir gently to mix with the onion and spices. Pour in 150 ml ($\frac{1}{4}$ pint) water and bring to the boil, then lower the heat and simmer, uncovered, for 10 minutes. Stir occasionally and add a few more spoonfuls of water if necessary.

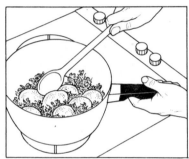

6 Fold the spinach gently into the potato mixture. Simmer for a further 5–10 minutes until the potatoes are just tender. Turn into a warmed serving dish and serve hot.

Menu Suggestion
The flavour of this curried spinach and potatoes goes well with most meat and poultry dishes, especially Gosht Madrasi (Beef Madras) page 40.

PIAZ AUR HARI MIRCH WALI BHINDI
(OKRA FRIED WITH ONION AND GREEN CHILLI)

0.30 £ 130 cals

HOT

Serves 4

450 g (1 lb) fresh okra, or two 425 g (15 oz) cans okra in brine, drained

45 ml (3 tbsp) ghee or vegetable oil

1 medium onion, skinned and finely sliced

2 small green chillies

10 ml (2 tsp) ground cumin

2.5 ml ($\frac{1}{2}$ tsp) salt

freshly ground pepper

2 Heat the oil in a large, heavy-based frying pan or wok, add the onion and fry over moderate heat, stirring constantly, for about 5 minutes until turning golden.

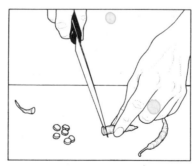

3 Meanwhile, trim the ends off the green chillies and cut the flesh into fine rings with a sharp knife. Remove as many seeds as you like, according to how hot the dish is to be.

4 Add the okra, chillies, cumin, salt and pepper to taste to the pan. Continue cooking over moderate heat, stirring constantly, for about 10–15 minutes. The fresh okra should be cooked but still quite crisp and the onions a deeper brown. The canned okra will become slightly sticky. Taste and adjust the seasoning, then turn into a warmed serving dish.

Menu Suggestion
Okra goes well with any dal dish (pages 97–105) and Khumbi Pullao (Mushroom Pilau) page 111 in a vegetarian menu. For meat eaters, the flavour of okra is especially good with lamb curries.

PIAZ AUR HARI MIRCH WALI BHINDI

Bhindi, translated as okra or ladies' fingers, are a long, thin tapering vegetable which are used extensively in Indian cooking. When trimming the ends in step 1, take care not to cut the flesh or a sticky substance will be released during cooking.

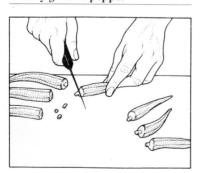

1 Wash the fresh okra and trim the ends. Dry well on absorbent kitchen paper. If using canned okra, rinse, drain and dry.

HARE SEM AUR NARIYAL
(GREEN BEANS WITH COCONUT)

0.30	£	200 cals

MILD

Serves 4

450 g (1 lb) French beans

salt and freshly ground pepper

450 g (1 lb) tomatoes

1 medium onion, skinned

115 g (4½ oz) desiccated coconut

45 ml (3 tbsp) ghee or vegetable oil

1 garlic clove, skinned and
   crushed

10 ml (2 tsp) garam masala
   (page 140)

30 ml (2 tbsp) tomato purée

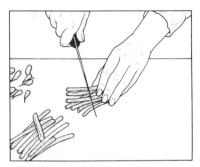

1 Top, tail and halve the French beans. Cook in a saucepan of boiling salted water for about 5 minutes or until just tender. Drain.

2 Roughly chop the tomatoes. Finely chop the onion. Place 100 g (4 oz) of the coconut in a measuring jug. Make up to 450 ml (¾ pint) with boiling water. Stir and leave to stand for 5 minutes. Strain through a sieve, pressing the coconut to squeeze out any liquid. Discard the contents of the sieve and reserve the coconut milk for later use.

3 Heat the ghee in a large, heavy-based frying pan, add the onion and fry gently for about 5 minutes until soft and lightly coloured.

4 Stir in the crushed garlic and garam masala and cook for 1–2 minutes, stirring. Add the coconut milk with the tomatoes, tomato purée and salt and pepper to taste. Bring to the boil, then boil the mixture rapidly, uncovered, for about 5 minutes.

5 Add the drained beans. Cook over gentle heat for 3–4 minutes, stirring occasionally, until heated through. Meanwhile, toast the remaining coconut under a preheated hot grill until golden. Taste and adjust seasoning, then turn into a warmed serving dish and sprinkle with the toasted coconut. Serve immediately.

Menu Suggestion

These green beans are mild in flavour, and are particularly good with hot curries such as Gosht Madrasi (Beef Madras) page 40 and Vindaloo (Hot Spicy Pork) page 50.

MUTTAR PANEER
(PEAS WITH CHEESE)

| 0.45 | 🍴 | 355 cals |

MEDIUM-HOT

Serves 4

350 g (12 oz) pressed paneer (page 154), whey reserved

100 ml (4 fl oz) vegetable oil

2 medium onions, skinned and roughly chopped

2.5 cm (1 inch) piece of fresh root ginger, peeled and roughly chopped

1 garlic clove, skinned and crushed

5 ml (1 tsp) turmeric

5 ml (1 tsp) garam masala (page 140)

2.5 ml ($\frac{1}{2}$ tsp) chilli powder

350 g (12 oz) fresh or frozen peas

4 small tomatoes, skinned and finely chopped

salt

30 ml (2 tbsp) chopped fresh coriander

2 Add the cubes of paneer to the hot oil and fry until pale golden on all sides, turning once. Remove from the oil and drain on absorbent kitchen paper.

3 Pour off all but about 60 ml (4 tbsp) of the oil. Add the onions, ginger and garlic and fry gently, stirring frequently, for 10 minutes. Add the turmeric, garam masala and chilli powder and fry for a further 2 minutes.

4 Add the peas and tomatoes to the pan and stir to combine with the spiced onion mixture. Add 100 ml (4 fl oz) whey and salt to taste, then cover tightly and simmer gently for 15 minutes or until the peas are tender.

1 Cut the pressed paneer into small cubes, reserving any whey. Heat the vegetable oil in a deep, heavy-based frying pan until very hot.

5 Add the paneer and coriander; shake the pan gently to mix the cheese with the peas. Simmer for a further 5 minutes.

Menu Suggestion
Serve as a vegetarian main course with Indian bread and a dal dish.

PHOOL GOBI KI BHAJI
(CAULIFLOWER IN CURRY SAUCE)

| 0.30 | £ | 240 cals |

MEDIUM-HOT

Serves 4

1 large cauliflower

90 ml (6 tbsp) ghee or vegetable oil

5 ml (1 tsp) black mustard seeds

5 ml (1 tsp) cumin seeds

5 cm (2 inch) piece of fresh root
  ginger, peeled and finely
  chopped

1 small onion, skinned and finely
  chopped

5 ml (1 tsp) salt

5 ml (1 tsp) turmeric

3 tomatoes, skinned and finely
  chopped

1 small green chilli, seeded and
  finely chopped

2.5 ml ($\frac{1}{2}$ tsp) sugar

30 ml (2 tbsp) chopped fresh
  coriander

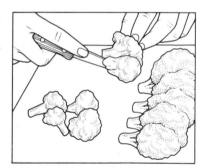

1 Divide the cauliflower into
small florets, discarding the
green leaves and tough stalks.
Wash the florets well and dry on
absorbent kitchen paper.

2 Heat the ghee in a heavy-based
saucepan or flameproof
casserole. Add the mustard seeds
and, when they begin to pop, stir
in the cumin seeds, ginger, onion,
salt and turmeric. Fry for 2–3
minutes, stirring constantly.

3 Add the cauliflower and mix
well to coat with the spice
mixture. Stir in the tomatoes,
chopped green chilli, sugar and
half of the chopped coriander.
Cover the pan tightly with a lid
and cook gently for 15 minutes or
until the cauliflower is tender but
not mushy.

4 Uncover the pan and boil
rapidly for 1–2 minutes to
thicken the sauce. Turn into a
warmed serving dish and sprinkle
with the remaining chopped
coriander. Serve immediately.

Menu Suggestion

Serve this curried cauliflower
with any dry meat or poultry main
course such as Bhoona Gosht (Dry
Beef Curry) page 43. Alternatively,
serve as part of a vegetarian meal
with Parathas or Puris (Shallow-
fried Unleavened Wholemeal
Bread or Deep-fried Unleavened
Wholemeal Bread) pages 144 and
142 and any dal dish (pages
97–105).

PHOOL GOBI KI BHAJI

This curry sauce can be used
for other vegetables besides
cauliflower. Potatoes (aloo) are
one of the best vegetables to
curry, and peas (muttar), okra
(bhindi), mushrooms (khumbi),
carrots (gajar) and aubergines
(baigan) are also good. They can
all be cooked in the same way as
the cauliflower in this recipe,
although the cooking time in
step 3 will vary according to
the type of vegetable used. Why
not choose three or four different
vegetables and make a mixed
vegetable curry?

SARSO AUR DAHI ME BHOONA HUA BAIGAN
(SAUTÉED AUBERGINES WITH MUSTARD SEEDS AND YOGURT)

0.45 £	135 cals

MILD

Serves 6

3 medium-sized aubergines, about 900 g (2 lb) total weight

60 ml (4 tbsp) ghee or vegetable oil

30 ml (2 tbsp) black mustard seeds, ground

2.5 ml ($\frac{1}{2}$ tsp) chilli powder

60 ml (4 tbsp) chopped fresh coriander

5 ml (1 tsp) salt

300 ml ($\frac{1}{2}$ pint) natural yogurt

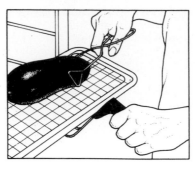

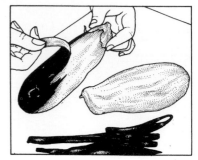

1 Put the aubergines under a preheated grill for about 15 minutes, turning occasionally. The aubergine skins should be black and charred and the flesh soft.

2 Leave the aubergines until just cool enough to handle, then peel the skins off and discard. Chop the flesh roughly.

3 Heat the ghee in a heavy-based frying pan, add the ground mustard seeds, chopped aubergine flesh and the chilli powder. Stir over moderate heat for about 5 minutes or until thoroughly hot, then add the coriander.

4 Beat the salt into the yogurt, then stir into the aubergine until evenly blended. Turn into a warmed serving dish and serve immediately.

Menu Suggestion
Mild in flavour, this aubergine and yogurt dish goes well with hot and spicy main courses, especially lamb and chicken.

SARSO AUR DAHI ME BHOONA HUA BAIGAN
Grilling whole aubergines until the skins char gives the flesh a wonderful smoky flavour. If you are making this dish in the summertime, the flavour will be even more accentuated if the aubergines are charred over a barbecue.

RASEDAR SABZI
(MIXED VEGETABLE CURRY)

1.20	✳	302 cals

HOT

Serves 4

50 ml (2 fl oz) ghee or vegetable oil

1 large onion, skinned and finely chopped

3 green chillies, seeded and finely chopped

5 ml (1 tsp) chilli powder

1.25 ml ($\frac{1}{4}$ tsp) turmeric

60 ml (4 tbsp) tomato purée

150 ml ($\frac{1}{4}$ pint) natural yogurt

225 g (8 oz) young turnips, peeled and sliced

225 g (8 oz) small carrots, peeled and diced

225 g (8 oz) cauliflower florets

600 ml (1 pint) coconut milk (page 134)

salt

225 g (8 oz) frozen peas

8 whole cloves

8 black peppercorns

seeds of 8 green cardamoms

10 ml (2 tsp) fennel seeds

1.25 ml ($\frac{1}{4}$ tsp) grated nutmeg

1 Heat the ghee in a heavy-based saucepan or flameproof casserole, add the onion and fry gently for about 5 minutes until soft and lightly coloured.

2 Add the chillies and stir to mix with the onion, then add the chilli powder and turmeric and fry, stirring, for 2 minutes.

3 Add the tomato purée and stir for a further 2 minutes, then add the yogurt, 15 ml (1 tbsp) at a time. Cook each addition over high heat, stirring constantly, until the yogurt is absorbed.

4 Add the turnips and carrots and fry, stirring frequently, for 5 minutes, then add the cauliflower and fry for 5 minutes more.

5 Gradually stir in the coconut milk and 300 ml ($\frac{1}{2}$ pint) water. Add salt to taste and bring to the boil. Lower the heat, cover and simmer for about 40 minutes until the vegetables are very tender, adding the peas for the last 10 minutes.

6 Meanwhile, dry fry the whole spices in a heavy-based frying pan for a few minutes, then grind to a fine powder in a small electric mill or with a pestle and mortar.

7 Remove the pan from the heat, sprinkle the ground spices and nutmeg over the vegetables and fold to mix. Cover the pan tightly with a lid, and remove from the heat. Leave to stand for 5 minutes, for the flavours to develop. Taste and adjust seasoning, turn into a warmed serving dish.

Menu Suggestion

This mixed vegetable curry is a most versatile dish. Serve it for a vegetarian main course with a dal dish (pages 97–105), Indian bread (pages 142–147), natural yogurt and Pudeene Ki Chutney (Mint Chutney) page 149. Alternatively, serve as a vegetable accompaniment with any fairly dry meat or fish main course.

BHALLE
(SPICED LENTIL CROQUETTES)

1.00* 🎩 £ 237 cals

MILD
* plus 24 hours soaking and 2 hours chilling

Serves 4

225 g (8 oz) moong dal (page 137)

5 ml (1 tsp) caraway seeds, crushed

2.5 ml (½ tsp) chilli powder

5 ml (1 tsp) garam masala
  (page 140)

2.5 ml (½ tsp) turmeric

salt

about 60 ml (4 tbsp) ghee or
  vegetable oil

300 ml (½ pint) natural yogurt

30 ml (2 tbsp) chopped fresh mint

freshly ground pepper

1 Pick over the dal and remove any grit or discoloured pulses. Put into a sieve and wash thoroughly under cold running water. Drain well.

2 Put the dal in a bowl and cover with cold water. Leave to soak for 24 hours.

3 Drain the dal, then work in batches in a food processor until ground to a fine paste. Add the spices and 2.5 ml (½ tsp) salt and work again until thoroughly mixed in.

4 Heat a little ghee in a heavy-based frying pan until smoking hot. Add spoonfuls of the croquette mixture and fry 2–3 minutes on each side until lightly coloured.

5 Remove the croquettes with a slotted spoon, then drain well on absorbent kitchen paper while frying the remainder. Add more ghee to the pan as necessary.

6 Put the yogurt in a blender or food processor with the mint and salt and pepper to taste. Work to a thin sauce.

7 Put the hot lentil cakes in a shallow serving dish and pour over the yogurt sauce. Cover the dish and chill for at least 2 hours before serving. Serve chilled.

Menu Suggestion
These lentil croquettes can be served as a starter or as a vegetarian main course, depending on the occasion. As a starter, they are substantial enough to be served on their own. As a main course they are excellent as part of a buffet-style spread with Rasedar Sabzi (Mixed Vegetable Curry) page 95, Rajma Dal (Red Kidney Beans with Ginger and Chilli) page 104, Khumbi Pullao (Mushroom Pilau) page 111, yogurt and a selection of Indian breads (pages 142–147), chutneys and pickles.

BHALLE
The moong dal in these croquettes are not cooked before being ground to a paste. For this reason it is absolutely essential to soak them for the full 24 hours or they will not be soft enough to grind.

Dal croquettes are extremely versatile. Served cold in this way with a yogurt sauce, they make an excellent starter or vegetarian main course. They can also be served hot without the sauce as a pre-dinner appetiser, in which case you may prefer to make them a little smaller so that they can be eaten easily with the fingers.

MASOOR KI DAL BAIGAN AUR KHUMBI
(MASOOR DAL WITH AUBERGINE AND MUSHROOMS)

| 1.00 | £ | ✳ | 190–252 cals |

MILD

Serves 6–8

350 g (12 oz) masoor dal
(page 137)

5 ml (1 tsp) turmeric

2 garlic cloves, skinned and
crushed

1 aubergine

225 g (8 oz) mushrooms, halved

5–10 ml (1–2 tsp) salt

2.5 ml ($\frac{1}{2}$ tsp) sugar

45 ml (3 tbsp) ghee or vegetable oil

5 ml (1 tsp) cumin seeds

5 ml (1 tsp) black mustard seeds

2.5 ml ($\frac{1}{2}$ tsp) fennel seeds

5 ml (1 tsp) garam masala
(page 140)

chopped fresh coriander,
to garnish

1 Pick over the dal and remove any grit or discoloured pulses. Put into a sieve and wash thoroughly under cold running water. Drain well.

2 Put the dal in a large saucepan with the turmeric and garlic. Cover with 1.4 litres (2$\frac{1}{2}$ pints) water. Bring to the boil and simmer for about 25 minutes.

3 Meanwhile, wash the aubergine and pat dry with absorbent kitchen paper. Cut into 2.5 cm (1 inch) cubes, discarding the ends.

4 Add the aubergine and mushrooms to the dal with the salt and sugar. Continue simmering gently for 15–20 minutes until all the vegetables are tender.

5 Heat the ghee in a separate small saucepan, add the remaining spices and fry for 1 minute or until the mustard seeds begin to pop.

6 Stir the spice mixture into the dal, cover the pan tightly with the lid and remove from the heat. Leave to stand for 5 minutes, for the flavours to develop. Turn into a warmed serving dish and garnish with coriander. Serve hot.

Menu Suggestion
Serve with Uble Chaval (Plain Boiled Rice) page 109 and Raita (Cucumber with Yogurt) page 152 for a vegetarian meal, or as an accompaniment to a meat or poultry main course.

MASOOR KI DAL BAIGAN AUR KHUMBI

While the dal is simmering in step 2, it is a good idea to dégorge the aubergine cubes.

Although not absolutely essential, this does help remove any bitter juices the aubergine may contain, especially if it is not a young vegetable and has many seeds in the flesh. Put the cubes in a colander and sprinkle with salt. Cover with a plate, put heavy weights on top to press the cubes down and extract the juices, then leave for about 20 minutes. Rinse under cold running water to remove the salt before adding the aubergines to the dal in step 4.

SOOKHI MOONG DAL
(DRY MOONG DAL)

0.50*	£	240–360 cals

MILD

* plus 4 hours soaking

Serves 4–6

225 g (8 oz) moong dal (page 137)

1 small onion, skinned

vegetable oil, for frying

10 ml (2 tsp) ground cumin

10 ml (2 tsp) ground coriander

1.25 ml (¼ tsp) turmeric

pinch of cayenne

salt

1 Pick over the dal and remove any grit or discoloured pulses. Put into a sieve and wash thoroughly under cold running water. Drain well. Put the dal into a bowl and cover with cold water. Leave to soak for about 4 hours.

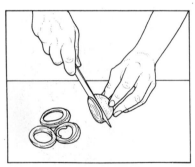

2 Meanwhile, cut the onion into very, very thin slices. Heat about 1 cm (½ inch) oil in a frying pan, add the onion and fry gently for about 10 minutes until golden brown.

3 Remove from the pan with a slotted spoon and spread on absorbent kitchen paper to drain. Leave to cool.

4 Drain the dal. Heat 30 ml (2 tbsp) oil in a large saucepan and stir in the cumin, coriander, turmeric and cayenne. Add the drained dal and stir together. Add 300 ml (½ pint) water and salt.

5 Bring to the boil, cover and simmer for about 25–30 minutes or until the dal is tender and the water absorbed.

6 Turn the dal into a warmed serving dish and sprinkle the crisp, browned onion over the top. Serve hot.

Menu Suggestion
Serve this spicy, dry pulse dish as part of a vegetarian meal with Sarso Aur Dahi Me Bhoona Hua Baigan (Sautéed Aubergines with Mustard Seeds and Yogurt) page 94 and any Indian bread (pages 142–147) or Pappar (Poppadoms) page 18.

ADRAK WALI CHANE KI DAL
(CHANNA DAL WITH GINGER)

1.15*	£	✳	330 cals

HOT

Serves 4

225 g (8 oz) channa dal (page 137)

25 g (1 oz) fresh root ginger

15 ml (1 tbsp) whole black peppercorns

60 ml (4 tbsp) ghee or vegetable oil

1 medium onion, skinned and chopped

1 garlic clove, skinned and crushed

10 ml (2 tsp) turmeric

about 1 litre (1¾ pints) chicken or vegetable stock

salt

1 Pick over the dal and remove any grit or discoloured pulses. Put into a sieve and wash thoroughly under cold running water. Drain well.

2 Peel the root ginger and chop the flesh finely. Crush the peppercorns with a pestle and mortar.

3 Heat the ghee in a heavy-based saucepan or flameproof casserole, add the onion and fry gently for about 5 minutes until soft and lightly coloured. Stir in the ginger, garlic, turmeric, peppercorns and dal. Stir over gentle heat for 2–3 minutes.

4 Add the stock and bring to the boil. Cover and simmer for about 1 hour, stirring frequently, until the dal is tender but still quite mushy in consistency. Add salt to taste before serving.

Menu Suggestion
For a vegetarian meal, serve with any rice dish (pages 107–113), Sag Aloo (Spinach and Potatoes) page 86, natural yogurt and a selection of pickles and relishes. Alternatively, serve as a vegetable accompaniment to any meat or poultry main course.

ADRAK WALI CHANE KI DAL
Take care that the stock used for cooking the dal is not salty, or this will prevent the pulse from becoming tender. Use home-made stock, as commercial stock cubes have a high salt content.

CHHOLE
(CHICK PEAS STEWED WITH TOMATOES)

| 0.25* | £ | 350 cals |

HOT

* plus overnight soaking and 2–3 hours boiling

Serves 4

225 g (8 oz) chhole (dried chick peas (page 137), or two 425 g (15 oz) cans chick peas, drained

4 garlic cloves, skinned and crushed

60 ml (4 tbsp) ghee or vegetable oil

2 medium onions, skinned and finely chopped

2 small green chillies, seeded and finely chopped

5 ml (1 tsp) turmeric

5 ml (1 tsp) paprika

15 ml (1 tbsp) ground cumin

15 ml (1 tbsp) ground coriander

5 ml (1 tsp) garam masala (page 140)

4 tomatoes, roughly chopped

30 ml (2 tbsp) chopped fresh coriander

15 ml (1 tbsp) chopped fresh mint

salt and freshly ground pepper

chopped fresh mint, to garnish

1 Wash the chick peas in several changes of water. Place in a large bowl, cover with plenty of fresh cold water and leave to soak overnight.

2 The next day, drain the chick peas and place in a large saucepan with half of the garlic. Cover with plenty of water, bring to the boil, cover and simmer for 2–3 hours until tender. Drain well and set aside.

3 Heat the ghee in a heavy-based saucepan or flameproof casserole, add the remaining garlic and the onions and fry gently for about 5 minutes until soft and lightly coloured. Add the chillies, turmeric, paprika, cumin, coriander and garam masala and fry, stirring, for a further 1–2 minutes.

4 Add the tomatoes, coriander and mint and cook, stirring, for 5–10 minutes until the tomatoes turn to a purée.

5 Add the cooked or canned chick peas and stir well. Simmer gently for another 5 minutes or until the chick peas are heated through. Add salt and pepper to taste, then turn into a warmed serving dish. Sprinkle with mint. Serve hot.

Menu Suggestion

Serve with any rice dish (pages 107–113) and natural yogurt, for a nutritious supper.

RAJMA DAL
(RED KIDNEY BEANS WITH GINGER AND CHILLI)

1.00*	£	267–400 cals

HOT

* plus overnight soaking

Serves 4–6

250 g (9 oz) rajma dal (dried red kidney beans—page 137), or two 425 g (15 oz) cans red kidney beans, drained

2–3 small green chillies

60 ml (4 tbsp) ghee or vegetable oil

2.5 cm (1 inch) piece of fresh root ginger, peeled and finely chopped

2 garlic cloves, skinned and crushed

150 ml ($\frac{1}{4}$ pint) single cream

60 ml (4 tbsp) tomato purée

salt and freshly ground pepper

fresh green chilli rings, to garnish

1 Wash the dried beans in several changes of water. Place in a large bowl, cover with plenty of fresh cold water and leave to soak overnight.

2 The next day, drain the beans and place in a large saucepan. Cover with plenty of water, bring to the boil and boil rapidly for 10 minutes. Reduce the heat, cover and simmer for about 30–40 minutes until tender.

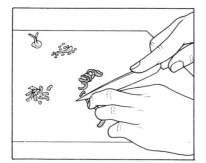

3 Meanwhile, halve and seed the chillies. Chop the flesh finely with a sharp knife. Rinse your hands thoroughly.

4 Heat the ghee in a heavy-based saucepan or flameproof casserole, add the ginger and garlic and fry gently for 2 minutes. Add the chopped chillies, the cream and tomato purée. Drain the kidney beans thoroughly and add to the pan. Stir well to mix.

5 Cook over gentle heat for 3–4 minutes or until thoroughly hot, stirring occasionally. Add salt and pepper to taste and turn into a warmed serving dish. Sprinkle with the chilli rings and serve hot.

Menu Suggestion
With their rich, creamy sauce, these red kidney beans go well with fairly dry meat dishes such as Bhoona Mhaans (Marinated Sautéed Steak) page 49 and Bhoona Gosht (Dry Beef Curry) page 43. For a vegetarian meal, they are best served with Uble Chaval (Plain Boiled Rice) page 109.

RAJMA DAL
It is essential to boil dried red kidney beans for a full 10 minutes at the beginning of their cooking time. This is to destroy a poisonous enzyme they contain, which can cause stomach upsets. This is not necessary with canned red kidney beans because they have already been boiled sufficiently. If you find pulses difficult to digest, a good tip is to drain off the water after it has first come to the boil, then start again with fresh cold water. This makes all pulses more easily digestible, and is well worth the few minutes extra time.

Rice

In this chapter you will find the pick of Indian rice dishes, from plain boiled rice to special occasion pullaos. In Indian cookery, every grain of rice should be separate, light and fluffy. Most Western cooks find this difficult to achieve, but if you follow the cooking methods in this chapter, you should have perfect rice every time.

MASALEDAL BASMATI
(SPICED FRIED BASMATI RICE)

0.30*	£	217–325 cals

* plus 30 minutes soaking

Serves 4–6

275 g (10 oz) basmati rice

30 ml (2 tbsp) ghee or vegetable oil

2.5 cm (1 inch) stick cinnamon

2 bay leaves

4 whole cloves

6 green cardamoms or 2 black cardamoms

2.5 ml ($\frac{1}{2}$ tsp) cumin seeds

2.5 ml ($\frac{1}{2}$ tsp) salt

1 Place the rice in a sieve and rinse under cold running water until the water runs clear. Transfer the rice to a bowl and cover with plenty of cold water. Leave to soak for 30 minutes.

2 Drain the rice well and leave to stand for 2 minutes. Heat the ghee in a heavy-based saucepan or flameproof casserole, add the cinnamon, bay leaves, cloves, cardamoms and cumin seeds and fry for 2 minutes, stirring constantly. Add the rice and salt and stir until well coated.

3 Level the rice and pour in enough water to come approximately 2.5 cm (1 inch) above the rice. Bring to the boil, cover tightly with a lid and cook very gently for 20 minutes. Do not stir or uncover the pan during cooking.

4 Remove the lid and carefully fluff up the rice with a fork. All of the water should have been absorbed and the rice should be tender. Taste and adjust seasoning, then transfer the rice to a warmed serving dish. Serve hot.

PEELAY CHAVAL
(YELLOW AROMATIC RICE)

| 0.35* | £ | 360–542 cals |

* plus 30 minutes soaking

Serves 4–6

275 g (10 oz) basmati rice

45 ml (3 tbsp) ghee or vegetable oil

1 onion, skinned and chopped

2 large garlic cloves, skinned and finely chopped

8 green cardamoms, crushed

salt and freshly ground pepper

about 450 ml ($\frac{3}{4}$ pint) hot chicken stock

100 g (4 oz) slivered almonds

orange or yellow food colouring

50 g (2 oz) sultanas

fresh coriander, to garnish

1 Place the rice in a sieve and rinse under cold running water until the water runs clear. Transfer the rice to a bowl and cover with plenty of cold water. Leave to soak for 30 minutes.

2 Heat 30 ml (2 tbsp) of the ghee in a large heavy-based saucepan or flameproof casserole, add the onion and garlic and fry gently for about 5 minutes until soft and lightly coloured.

3 Meanwhile, drain the rice well and leave to stand for 2 minutes. Add to the pan and fry, stirring, for 2 minutes or until the ghee is absorbed. Add the cardamoms and salt and pepper, then pour in enough hot stock to just cover the rice. DO NOT STIR. Bring to the boil, lower the heat, cover and simmer gently for 10 minutes.

4 Meanwhile, heat the remaining ghee in a separate pan. Add the almonds and fry until golden brown, shaking the pan constantly. Drain well.

5 Sprinkle a few drops of food colouring over the rice. DO NOT STIR. Cover again and simmer very gently for a further 5 minutes or until rice is tender.

6 Fork two-thirds of the almonds into the rice with the sultanas. Taste and adjust seasoning. Cover, turn off the heat and leave to stand for 5 minutes. Turn into a warmed serving dish and garnish.

UBLE CHAVAL
(PLAIN BOILED RICE)

0.30*	£	205 cals

* plus 30 minutes soaking

Serves 4

225 g (8 oz) basmati rice

2.5 ml ($\frac{1}{2}$ tsp) salt

1 Place the rice in a sieve and rinse under cold running water until the water runs clear. Transfer the rice to a bowl and cover with plenty of cold water. Leave to soak for 30 minutes.

2 Drain the rice well and leave to stand for 2 minutes. Place in a heavy-based saucepan or flame-proof casserole. Level the rice, sprinkle with the salt, and pour in enough water to come 2.5 cm (1 inch) above the rice.

3 Bring to the boil, cover tightly with a lid and cook very gently for 20 minutes. Do not uncover the pan during cooking.

4 Remove the lid and carefully fluff up the rice with a fork. All of the water should have been absorbed and the rice tender.

KHUMBI PULLAO
(MUSHROOM PILAU)

0.30*	£	242–323 cals

* plus 30 minutes soaking

Serves 6–8

450 g (1 lb) basmati rice

225 g (8 oz) button mushrooms

30 ml (2 tbsp) ghee or vegetable oil

12 green cardamoms

6 whole cloves

5–6 pieces cassia bark (page 139)

5 ml (1 tsp) salt

freshly ground pepper

1 Place the rice in a sieve and rinse under cold running water until the water runs clear. Transfer the rice to a bowl and cover with plenty of cold water. Leave to soak for 30 minutes.

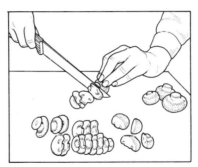

2 Wipe the mushrooms, then slice thinly. Heat the ghee in a large heavy-based saucepan or flameproof casserole, add the cardamoms, cloves and cassia bark with the mushrooms and fry over high heat for 1–2 minutes, stirring constantly.

3 Drain the rice well and leave to stand for 2 minutes. Remove the pan from the heat and stir in the rice. Add the salt and pepper to taste and mix well. Level the rice and pour in enough water to come approximately 2.5 cm (1 inch) above the rice.

4 Bring to the boil, cover tightly with a lid and cook very gently for 20 minutes. Do not uncover the pan during cooking.

5 Remove the lid and carefully fluff up the rice with a fork. All of the water should have been absorbed and the rice should be tender. Taste and adjust seasoning, then transfer the pilau to a warmed serving dish. Serve hot.

KHUMBI PULLAO
There are many different schools of thought on the preparation of rice for cooking. The method of rinsing and soaking used here has been tried and tested, and found to be especially good with basmati rice. Rinsing or washing under cold running water rids the rice of excess starch and any white polishing powder, and soaking helps ensure that the grains are separate and do not stick during cooking. Although both these processes may seem time-consuming, they are well worth it when you can be sure of perfect fluffy grains of rice, and the beautifully aromatic basmati, sometimes called the "king of rice", is too expensive to waste.

PULLAO
(FRUIT AND NUT PILAU)

0.40*	570 cals

* plus 30 minutes soaking

Serves 4

225 g (8 oz) basmati rice

50 g (2 oz) stoned dried apricots

50 g (2 oz) dried mango or peach

50 g (2 oz) shelled pistachio nuts

50 g (2 oz) unsalted cashew nuts

5 ml (1 tsp) cumin seeds

6 green cardamoms

8 black peppercorns

2 bay leaves

2.5 cm (1 inch) stick cinnamon

50 ml (2 fl oz) ghee or vegetable oil

1 large onion, skinned and finely chopped

good pinch of saffron threads, or 2.5 ml ($\frac{1}{2}$ tsp) turmeric

salt and freshly ground pepper

1 Place the rice in a sieve and rinse under cold running water until the water runs clear. Transfer the rice to a bowl and cover with plenty of cold water. Leave to soak for 30 minutes.

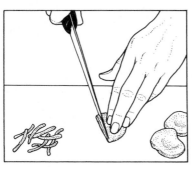

2 Meanwhile, prepare the fruit and nuts. Slice the apricots and mango or peach into thin slivers or slices.

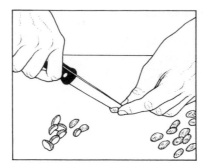

3 Split the pistachios in half lengthways. Leave the cashews whole. Grind the cumin, cardamoms, peppercorns, bay leaves and cinnamon in a small electric mill or with a pestle and mortar.

4 Heat the ghee in a heavy-based saucepan or flameproof casserole, add the onion and fry gently for about 5 minutes until soft and lightly coloured.

5 Drain the rice and leave to stand for 2 minutes. Meanwhile, add the crushed spices to the onion and fry, stirring, for 2 minutes. Add the rice and saffron with salt and pepper to taste and stir until the rice is well coated with spices.

6 Level the rice and pour in enough water to come approximately 2.5 cm (1 inch) above the rice. Bring to the boil.

7 Sprinkle the prepared dried fruit and nuts over the pan. Cover tightly with a lid and cook very gently for 20 minutes. Do not uncover the pan during cooking.

8 Remove the lid and carefully fluff up the rice with a fork, mixing in the fruit and nuts. All of the water should have been absorbed and the rice should be tender. Taste and adjust seasoning, then transfer the rice to a warmed serving dish. Serve hot.

PULLAO

There is often confusion between pullaos and biryanis: A pullao is quicker to make than a biryani, and it has less fat, so it is a lighter dish altogether. Biryanis are really meals in themselves, in which other ingredients such as meat and vegetables often weigh twice as much as the rice. A biryani is also usually heavy with spices and butter or ghee.

Amongst the many different types of pullao (often spelt pilau), there is the plain and simple sadah pullao, sweet pullaos for dessert, and shahi or royal pullaos which contain special ingredients and are usually reserved for festivals and celebrations. The pullao on this page falls into the category of shahi pullaos, with its exotic dried fruit, pistachio nuts and saffron.

Dried mango and peach are now widely available at health food shops, large supermarkets and delicatessens; they are absolutely delicious, and well worth looking for.

Desserts and Sweetmeats

Indian sweet dishes are invariably oversweet for most Western tastes, and the recipes in this chapter have been adapted using less sugar. Although in the West we are accustomed to eating sweets and desserts at the end of most meals, this is rarely the case in India. Desserts and sweetmeats are reserved for special occasions, festivals and other celebrations. Everyday Indian meals usually finish with fresh fruit such as mangoes, melons and guavas.

PISTA AUR BADAM KI KULFI
(PISTACHIO AND ALMOND ICE CREAM)

| 1.30* | 🗆 £ £ ✳ | 480 cals |

* plus 5 hours freezing

Serves 6

1.4 litres (2½ pints) milk

15 ml (1 tbsp) rice flour

175 g (6 oz) granulated sugar

25 g (1 oz) pistachio nuts

50 g (2 oz) ground almonds

few drops of rose water

150 ml (¼ pint) double cream

shredded pistachio nuts,
    to decorate

1 Pour the milk into a large, heavy-based saucepan. Bring to the boil, then simmer gently for about 45 minutes or until the milk reduces by half. Cool slightly.

2 Mix the rice flour with a little of the cooled milk until smooth. Return to the pan and bring to the boil, stirring. Cook for 15 minutes, stirring frequently until a thin batter. Strain, add the sugar and stir until dissolved. Cool.

3 Cover the pistachio nuts with boiling water. Leave to stand for 1–2 minutes, then drain.

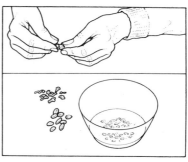

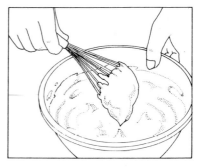

4 Ease the skins off the pistachios with the fingers. Shred the nuts finely. Stir the pistachios, ground almonds and rose water into the milk mixture.

5 Whip the cream lightly, then fold into the mixture. Pour into a shallow freezer container.

6 Freeze the mixture for at least 5 hours until firm. Whisk occasionally during this time — this is important to break down the ice crystals.

7 Allow the ice cream to soften in the refrigerator for about 1 hour before serving. Serve in scoops or cut into slices, decorated with shredded pistachios.

Menu Suggestion
This is a very special ice cream, traditionally served at wedding banquets in India. It is best reserved for dinner parties, but only serve it after a fairly light main course as it is very rich.

AAM KI KULFI
(MANGO ICE CREAM)

| 0.30* | 🗒 | ✳ | 399–598 cals |

* plus 1 hour cooling and 5–6
hours freezing

Serves 4–6

450 ml (¾ pint) milk

1 vanilla pod

4 egg yolks

75 g (3 oz) sugar

2 ripe mangoes, skinned and
    puréed, or two 425 g (15 oz)
    cans mango slices, drained and
    puréed

juice of 1 lime

300 ml (½ pint) double cream

twists of fresh lime, to decorate
    (optional)

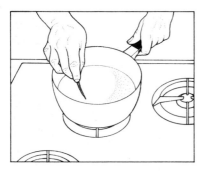

1 Pour the milk into a large,
heavy-based saucepan. Add
the vanilla pod and bring almost to
the boil. Remove from the heat,
cover and leave to infuse for at
least 15 minutes. Remove the
vanilla pod.

2 Put the egg yolks and sugar in
a large bowl and beat together.
Stir in the milk, then strain back
into the pan.

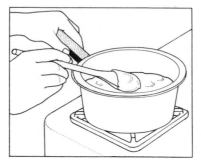

3 Cook the custard gently,
stirring, until it coats the back
of a wooden spoon. Do not boil.
Cool completely for at least 1 hour.

4 Stir the mango purée and lime
juice into the cool custard.
Whip the cream lightly, then fold
into the mixture. Pour into a
shallow freezer container.

5 Freeze the mixture for about
2 hours until mushy in texture.
Turn into a large, chilled bowl
and mash with a fork. Freeze for
3–4 hours until firm.

6 Soften in the refrigerator for
about 1 hour before serving,
decorated, if liked.

Menu Suggestion
Mango ice cream is very rich.
Serve at a dinner party.

Do not whip the fresh cream if
using a mechanical churn or ice
cream maker. Agitate the chilled
custard and unwhipped cream
together.

Taze Phal Ka Salat
(FRESH FRUIT SALAD)

| 0.20 | f | 88–117 cals |

Serves 6–8

3 ripe peaches

2 ripe guavas

2 ripe bananas

45 ml (3 tbsp) caster sugar

2.5 ml (½ tsp) salt

freshly ground pepper

5 ml (1 tsp) cumin seeds, dry fried (page 140)

30 ml (2 tbsp) lemon or lime juice

pinch of cayenne

sprigs of mint, to decorate

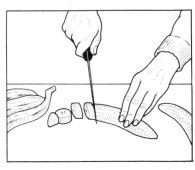

4 Peel the bananas, cut into chunks, then mix carefully with the peaches, guavas and remaining ingredients. Serve immediately, decorated with sprigs of mint.

Menu Suggestion
This Indian fruit salad is cool and refreshing, the perfect dessert to serve at the end of any hot and spicy meal.

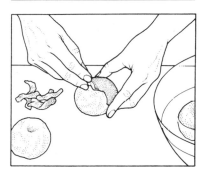

1 Skin the peaches. Plunge them into a bowl of boiling water, leave for 30 seconds, then remove the skins.

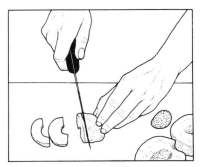

2 Cut the skinned peaches in half and remove the stones. Slice the peach flesh thinly and place in a serving bowl.

3 Cut the guavas in half, scoop out the seeds and discard them. Peel the halved guavas, then slice them neatly and add to the peaches in the bowl.

TAZE PHAL KA SALAT
Fresh guavas are available at specialist greengrocers, Indian stores and some of the larger supermarkets. Guavas are a tropical fruit, originally from South America, with a pretty creamy-pink skin. The flesh has a delicately scented aroma and a most delicious flavour. The seeds in the centre are not edible and should be removed before serving the fruit. Fresh guavas are often eaten at the end of an Indian meal as they are most refreshing, and ice creams and water ices made with guavas are especially suitable for desserts after an Indian meal. If you cannot get fresh guavas, use canned guavas in this recipe; they make a good substitute in a fruit salad because they have a good colour.

KESAR WALI DAHI
(BAKED SAFFRON YOGURT)

1.00* £	250 cals

* plus cooling and chilling

Serves 8

300 ml (½ pint) milk

pinch of saffron threads

6 green cardamoms

2 eggs

2 egg yolks

383 g (13.5 oz) can condensed milk

300 ml (½ pint) natural yogurt

1 large ripe mango, to decorate

1 Bring the milk, saffron and cardamoms to the boil. Remove from the heat, cover and infuse for 10–15 minutes.

2 Put the eggs, egg yolks, condensed milk and yogurt in a bowl and beat together.

3 Strain in the milk, stirring gently to mix. Divide between 8 ramekin dishes in a roasting tin.

4 Add hot water to come halfway up the sides. Bake in the oven at 180°C (350°F) mark 4 until firm to the touch.

5 Cool the baked yogurt desserts completely, then chill for at least 2 hours before serving.

6 To serve, run a blunt-edged knife around the edge of each yogurt, then turn out on to individual dishes.

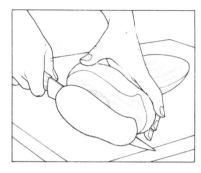

7 Peel the skin off the mango sections. Slice thinly on either side of the central stone. Serve with the saffron yogurts.

Menu Suggestion
These individual, golden-tinted yogurts make an attractive finale to an Indian meal. They are also excellent for children at tea-time, served with fresh fruit.

KESAR WALI DAHI
Mango is a tropical fruit which has been grown in India for centuries, but it is now grown in other tropical countries throughout the world. In India, fresh ripe mangoes are eaten raw at the end of a meal, or made into ice creams and sorbets. Dried mango powder is used in cooking, and mango chutney is one of the best-known Indian condiments. Look for fresh mangoes in specialist greengrocers and supermarkets: their skin can be any colour from green to yellow or red. The ripe fruit should be soft to the touch but still slightly firm—never squashy or bruised.

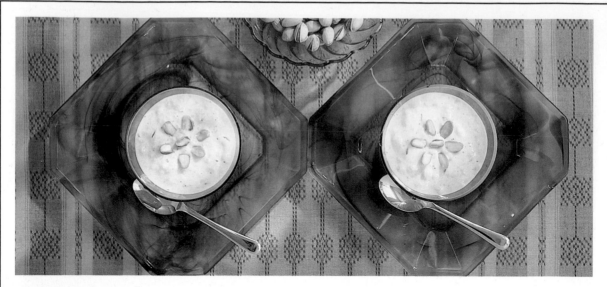

KHEER
(CHILLED CREAMED RICE)

1.15*	270–404 cals

* plus cooling and at least 2 hours chilling

Serves 4–6

seeds of 4 green cardamoms

4 whole cloves

2.5 cm (1 inch) stick cinnamon

1.2 litres (2 pints) milk

75 g (3 oz) short grain 'pudding' rice

100 g (4 oz) caster sugar

1.25 ml ($\frac{1}{4}$ tsp) orange flower water

varak (page 158), shelled and split pistachio nuts or slivered blanched almonds, to decorate

1 Grind the cardamom seeds, whole cloves and cinnamon stick in a small electric mill or with a pestle and mortar to a coarse powder.

2 Pour the milk into a heavy-based saucepan, add the rice, sugar and crushed spices and bring slowly to the boil, stirring.

3 Lower the heat and simmer very gently, uncovered, for 1 hour or until the rice is tender. Stir frequently during this time to prevent the rice sticking to the bottom of the pan.

4 Remove the pan from the heat and pour the Kheer into a bowl. Add the orange flower water and stir well to mix.

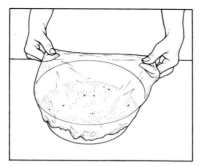

5 Cover the bowl with cling film. Leave until cold, then chill for at least 2 hours before serving.

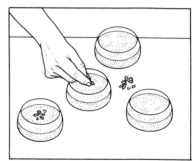

6 To serve, pour the Kheer into 4–6 individual glasses or glass dishes and decorate with varak, pistachios or almonds. Serve well chilled.

Menu Suggestion
Kheer makes an elegant dinner party dessert. If liked, the top of each glass can be flooded with fresh cream and the nuts floated on top.

GAJAR HALVA
(SWEET CARROT PUDDING)

| 3.00 | 🍳 | £ | 411–617 cals |

Serves 4–6

450 g (1 lb) carrots

750 ml (1¼ pints) milk

150 ml (¼ pint) single cream

75 g (3 oz) granulated sugar

15 ml (1 tbsp) treacle

45 ml (3 tbsp) ghee or melted butter

100 g (4 oz) ground almonds

seeds of 6 green cardamoms, crushed

25 g (1 oz) sultanas

chopped pistachios, to decorate

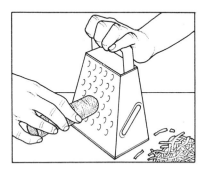

1 Peel the carrots, grate roughly and put into a large, heavy-based saucepan. Pour in the milk and cream and bring to the boil, stirring constantly.

2 Simmer gently, stirring occasionally to prevent any sticking, for at least 2 hours until the milk has evaporated and the mixture is greatly reduced.

3 Stir in the sugar and treacle, then simmer for a further 30 minutes, stirring occasionally to prevent sticking.

4 Add the ghee, ground almonds, crushed cardamom seeds and sultanas. Cook, stirring, for another 5–10 minutes until the mixture begins to look oily on the surface.

5 Transfer to a serving dish and decorate with the pistachio nuts. Serve hot or cold.

Menu Suggestion
This carrot pudding is rich and filling, best reserved for a winter meal. It can be served with single cream if liked, but if it is to be served cold, it is best served on its own.

GULAB JAMUN
(DEEP-FRIED MILK BALLS IN CARDAMOM SYRUP)

| 1.00 | ☐ | £ | 425–638 cals |

Serves 4–6

225 g (8 oz) granulated sugar

6 green cardamoms, lightly crushed

175 g (6 oz) dried skimmed milk with vegetable fat

10 ml (2 tsp) baking powder

50 g (2 oz) self raising flour

15 ml (1 tbsp) semolina

about 150 ml (¼ pint) milk

vegetable oil, for deep-frying

rose water (optional)

1 Put the sugar in a saucepan with 450 ml (¾ pint) water. Bring slowly to the boil, stirring to dissolve the sugar. Add the crushed cardamoms and boil rapidly for 4 minutes. Remove from the heat, cover and set aside.

2 In a bowl, mix together the dried milk, baking powder, flour, semolina and enough milk to mix to a stiff dough rather like shortcrust pastry.

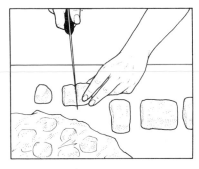

3 Turn out on to a board and knead the dough until smooth, then divide into 24 pieces. Keep covered with cling film to prevent the dough drying out.

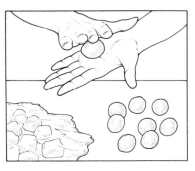

4 Roll each piece of dough into a completely smooth ball. Meanwhile, heat the oil in a deep-fat fryer to 170°C (325°F).

5 Deep-fry the dough pieces in batches for 2–3 minutes until golden brown on all sides, turning them with a slotted spoon to ensure even browning. They must not fry too quickly as they have to cook all the way through before becoming too brown on the outside.

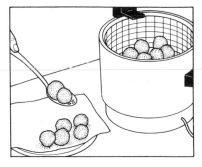

6 Remove them from the oil with a slotted spoon and drain on absorbent kitchen paper while frying the remainder.

7 While the Gulab Jamuns are still hot, transfer them to a serving dish. Pour over the warm syrup and sprinkle with rose water, if liked. Serve this dessert warm or cold.

Menu Suggestion
This is a very sweet and very rich dessert. Serve for a special dinner party, with single cream for the self-indulgent!

GULAB JAMUN
Gulab Jamun are very popular in India; they are *very* sweet and syrupy, with a wonderfully exotic aroma of rose water, which is worth adding at the end if you want your Gulab Jamun to be as authentic as possible. Rose water is available in bottles at chemists, delicatessens and herbalists. For a pretty touch, sprinkle them with a few fresh rose petals — pink or apricot petals look especially attractive.

MEETHE CHAWAL
(SWEET INDIAN RICE PUDDING WITH ALMONDS, RAISINS AND COCONUT)

| 1.10 | 527–790 cals |

Serves 4–6

175 g (6 oz) long grain rice

2.5 ml (½ tsp) salt

100 g (4 oz) sugar

2.5 cm (1 inch) stick cinnamon

120 ml (8 tbsp) ghee or melted butter

seeds of 4 green cardamoms

1.25 ml (¼ tsp) grated nutmeg

pinch of saffron threads

100 g (4 oz) slivered blanched almonds

100 g (4 oz) raisins

50 g (2 oz) desiccated coconut

single cream, to serve (optional)

1 Bring a large saucepan of water to the boil. Add the rice and salt and bring back to the boil. Stir once, then simmer, uncovered, for 10 minutes.

2 Meanwhile, put the sugar and cinnamon stick in a separate heavy-based saucepan. Add 300 ml (½ pint) water and heat gently until the sugar has dissolved. Bring to the boil, then boil rapidly for 1 minute. Remove from the heat.

3 Drain the rice. Heat the ghee in a flameproof casserole, add the rice, cardamoms and nutmeg and cook gently, stirring, for 1–2 minutes until the rice glistens.

4 Add the sugar syrup (with the cinnamon stick) to the rice and stir gently to mix. Sprinkle in the saffron and stir again.

5 Cover the pan tightly with a lid and cook in the oven at 180°C (350°F) mark 4 for 40 minutes. Discard the cinnamon stick and cover the casserole tightly again. Leave to stand for 5 minutes, then stir in the nuts, raisins and coconut. Spoon into individual dishes and serve immediately with the single cream if liked.

Menu Suggestion

In India, hot sweet rice dishes such as this one are served with cream, called malai. The rice is very rich and sweet because of the butter and sugar, and for most Western tastes cream is hardly necessary. For a special occasion, you may like to serve the pudding with whipped cream, which can be made lighter by folding in a stiffly whisked egg white after whipping.

MEETHE CHAWAL

When buying cardamoms for sweet dishes such as this rice pudding, check that they are the green rather than the black variety. Green cardamoms have pale green husks with black seeds inside—it is the colour of the husk that is important. Green cardamoms have a fine, delicate aroma and taste, whereas black cardamoms are stronger in flavour and coarser in texture— more suited to savoury dishes. Green cardamoms are used frequently in Indian desserts because they have digestive properties, and they are often chewed raw after hot, spicy curries, to aid digestion and help sweeten the breath.

BADAM KI BURFI
(ALMOND SWEETMEAT)

1.00* £ £ 130 cals

* plus 25–35 minutes cooling

Makes about 24

15 ml (1 tbsp) ghee or melted butter

900 ml (1½ pints) milk

225 g (8 oz) granulated sugar

225 g (8 oz) ground almonds or pistachios (see box)

1.25 ml (¼ tsp) almond flavouring or 2.5 ml (½ tsp) rose water

24 whole blanched almonds, to decorate

1 Grease a 28 × 18 cm (11 × 7 inch) rectangular tin with a little of the ghee. Set aside.

2 Pour the milk into a large, heavy-based saucepan and bring to the boil. Boil rapidly for about 20–30 minutes, stirring occasionally, until reduced to the thickness of double cream. Strain the milk and return to a clean saucepan.

3 Add the sugar, stir well and simmer for 10 minutes. Add the ground nuts and cook for a further 10 minutes, stirring all the time. Do not let the mixture catch or burn.

4 Stir in the remaining ghee and cook stirring all the time until the mixture begins to come away from the sides of the pan.

5 Remove the pan from the heat and stir in a few drops of almond flavouring or rose water.

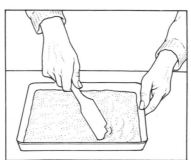

6 Pour the mixture into the prepared tin and spread flat with a spatula. Leave the mixture to cool for 25 minutes.

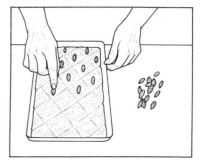

7 Cut into 24 diamonds, then press 1 almond into each diamond. Leave to cool and harden completely before serving.

Menu Suggestion
Serve these sweetmeats as a snack at any time of day, or with coffee or tea after an Indian meal.

BADAM KI BURFI

Do not buy ready-ground nuts for this sweetmeat; it is much better to buy whole nuts and grind them yourself just before you need them—they will release their natural oils and have far more flavour. Ready-ground nuts are always dry in comparison with those you have ground at home. Grind blanched almonds or shelled pistachios finely in a nut grinder, or in a blender or food processor.

USEFUL INFORMATION AND BASIC RECIPES

How to Plan an Indian Meal

With such a vast range of dishes to choose from, planning a balanced Indian meal can be baffling. The following chapter guides you through the pitfalls and gives you some rules to follow. There is also a selection of sample menus, for both vegetarian and non-vegetarian meals.

EATING INDIAN STYLE

Most Indians like to eat with their hands, using the Indian breads to scoop up the curries and rice or to wrap around a kebab. When entertaining foreign guests, however, spoons, forks and plates will often be offered. Indian breads such as nan and chapatis are easiest to eat with the fingers, and are excellent for mopping up all the delicious juices from the curries.

Traditional serving tray and bowls

For most occasions, the thali will be used. This round flat tray contains bowls (katoris) of rice, dals and curries, while the breads and other dry foods are placed directly on the thali. In South India, fresh banana leaves often replace the thali. Clay cups are also used to serve various curries, yogurt and dals. These are only used once and are thrown away after the meal. Hindus consider crockery and cutlery that is used again and again unhygienic.

PLANNING AN INDIAN MEAL

An Indian meal generally consists of a meat dish, a vegetable dish, a dal, yogurt (either plain or as a relish), bread and/or rice, and possibly a salad. Pickles or chutneys may also be offered. Indian meals place the emphasis on rice or bread; the rich spicy flavours of the meat, fish or dals are best appreciated against the bland background they provide. The main dishes will be carefully balanced to include some dry curries and other more liquid dishes. A soup may be included in the meal; it will not be served as a first course, but will be served with the other dishes. Vegetarian meals will also be based on rice or bread, often both. Vegetarians should increase the number of dals and vegetable dishes, and some sort of yogurt should always be included in a vegetarian meal. Lentils or dried beans and green vegetables will be offered, some liquid, some dry. Spiced fresh cheese, yogurt or buttermilk will also often be included, and each diner will have their own bowl of natural yogurt.

HOW TO EAT AN INDIAN MEAL

Rice is served first in the centre of the plate and a little of each of the various other dishes placed around

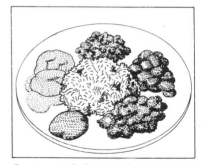

Serving an Indian meal

it. The rice should not be mixed together with the other dishes. One curry should be tasted with each mouthful of rice in order to appreciate the characteristics of each dish. Very liquid curries may be spooned on top of a little of the rice, leaving the remaining rice plain to be eaten with other dishes. Very liquid dishes that are to be eaten with bread are served in small individual bowls.

WHAT TO DRINK

Indians generally drink only iced water with their meals. Carbonated drinks are avoided as they tend to bring out the burning sensation of hot dishes. Fine wines are lost against the many flavours of the spiced dishes, although a semi-sweet white or rosé wine can be good. Try fruit juices or fruit punch, chilled beer, home-made lemonade or lassi, an Indian yogurt drink. Spiced Indian tea makes a good hot drink alternative.

DESSERTS

Most Indian meals end with fresh fruit. Mangoes are a great favourite, or try papaya, water-melon or guavas. Made-up desserts are reserved for special occasions, banquets or feast days; such Indian desserts are exceed-ingly sweet, with a concentrated flavour. They are often based on condensed milk or almonds and are considered beneficial to health. Desserts are not necessarily served at the end of a meal. They can be eaten at the beginning, or placed on the thali and eaten at any time during the meal.

MENUS

The following menus will each serve four to six people:

NON-VEGETARIAN MENU
Dal Ka Shorva *(Lentil Soup)*
Korma Sheer *(Pork Chops with Almond Milk)*
Rasedar Sabzi *(Mixed Vegetable Curry)*
Peelay Chaval *(Yellow Aromatic Rice)*
Cachumber *(Tomato, Onion and Coriander Relish)*
Gajar Halva *(Sweet Carrot Pudding)*

NON-VEGETARIAN MENU
Tikka Murgh *(Chicken Tikka)*
Nan *(Flat Leavened White Bread)*
Bhoona Gosht *(Dry Beef Curry)*
Phool Gobi Ki Bhaji *(Cauliflower in Curry Sauce)*
Pudeene Ki Chutney *(Mint Chutney)*

NON-VEGETARIAN MENU
Bhalle *(Spiced Lentil Croquettes)*
Masale Wala Jhinga *(Butterfly Prawns)*
Gosht Biryani *(Spiced Lamb and Rice Casserole)*
Piaz Aur Hari Mirch Wali Bhindi *(Okra Fried with Onion and Green Chilli)*
Adrak Wali Chane Ki Dal *(Channa Dal with Ginger)*
Chapatis *(Unleavened Wholemeal Bread)*
Pista Aur Badam Ki Kulfi *(Pistachio and Almond Ice Cream)*

VEGETARIAN MENU
Sabzi Ke Samose *(Vegetable Samosas)*
Sem Aur Nariyal Ki Bhaji *(Green Beans with Coconut)*
Masaledar Dal *(Spiced Dal)*
Tale Hua Aloo *(Fried Masala Potatoes)*
Salat *(Indian Salad)*
Dahi *(Yogurt)*
Sag Paratha *(Spinach Paratha)*

VEGETARIAN MENU
Phool Gobi Ki Bhaji *(Cauliflower in Curry Sauce)*
Muttar Paneer *(Peas with Cheese)*
Sag Aloo *(Potato with Spinach)*
Chhole *(Spiced Chick Peas)*
Pilau Hazur Pasandh *(Rice Cooked with Peas and Vegetables)*
Dahi/Raita *(Yogurt/Cucumber with Yogurt)*
Aam Ki Kulfi *(Mango Ice Cream)*

VEGETARIAN MENU
Masaledar Dal Ka Shorva *(Spiced Dal Soup)*
Sookhi Moong Dal *(Dry Moong Dal)*
Sarso Aur Dahi Me Bhoona Hua Baigan *(Sautéed Aubergine Cooked with Mustard Seeds and Yogurt)*
Salat *(Indian Salad)*
Sag Paratha *(Spinach Paratha)*
Masaledal Basmati *(Spiced Fried Basmati Rice)*
Taze Phal Ka Salat *(Fresh Fruit Salad)*

Indian Cooking Styles

The main culinary styles of Indian cooking are described in this chapter. Use it as a reference when trying out the recipes in the book to give you a better understanding of the techniques involved. A brief description of some of the special Indian equipment used is also given here.

Methods of cooking in India vary greatly from region to region. There are, however, several cooking styles and techniques which are commonly used.

BHOONA (Frying)
This is a gentle process whereby dry spices or moist onions, garlic and ginger are fried until golden. The mixture is stirred constantly to prevent over browning and to stop the ingredients from sticking to the pan. When frying onion and spices, the onion is cooked first until golden, then the spices are added until they have released their flavour into the ghee or oil. At this stage the meat, fish or vegetables are added, stirring well.

DOPIAZA
This is a variation on a korma (see below), in which two lots of onions are used (the word dopiaza means 'two onions'). Half of the onions are browned in the ghee or oil before adding the meat. Towards the end of the cooking time, the second half of the onions are added to give a different texture and taste to the dish.

DUM (Pot Roasting)
The word dum describes the steam created inside a heavy cooking pot with a well-fitting lid. Meat, poultry and rice dishes are cooked in this way. Traditionally, the lid of the pan was sealed with a dough paste to trap all the steam. A special dumming pot has a concave lid where hot coals or water are placed, thereby heating

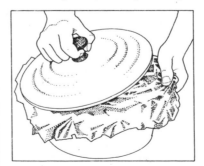

Foil under a casserole lid

the food from the top and bottom. All the flavour of the food is then concentrated and the steam helps to tenderise meat and poultry. A similar effect can be achieved by placing foil under a tight fitting lid of a casserole dish.

KORMA (Braising)
This technique is used in cooking in the Northern and Central parts of India. It is particularly important in Muglai dishes. Korma is meat or vegetables braised with stock, yogurt or cream until rich and thick. Meat or poultry is often marinated in yogurt and spices first, then cooked gently in some of the marinade ingredients.

MARINATING
Meat and fish are slashed or cut into small pieces and left to marinate in yogurt and seasonings.

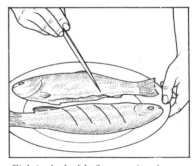

Fish is slashed before marinating

Yogurt helps to tenderise the food and the spicy flavours penetrate deep into the flesh. Chicken is always skinned before being marinated. The meat is then grilled, baked or cooked in the tandoor.

TALAWA (Deep-frying)
Talawa food is crisp, light and with no greasy taste, if properly cooked. Vegetables, small pieces of meat or fish and sweet mixtures are coated in batter or crumbs before being deep-fried in ghee or oil.

TANDOORI

A tandoor is a large clay oven heated to high temperatures by charcoal. Meat, fish and other foods are marinated before being lowered into the oven on skewers to bake. The special qualities of

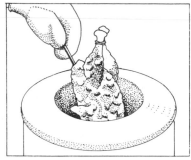

Lower the chicken on skewers

the oven ensure the food is crisp on the outside and moist and tender inside. A type of flat bread called nan, which is pressed on to the walls of the oven to bake, is the usual accompaniment to tandoori food. A barbecue or rotisserie is the best substitute for this special clay oven.

TARKA

This is a spicy topping poured over a dish immediately before it is served. It is usually reserved for dishes made with lentils. Aromatic spices such as cumin or mustard seeds, cloves, garlic or cardamoms, are fried quickly in very hot ghee or sesame oil until the spices turn brown. The mixture is then poured over the dal while it sizzles.

Tarka being poured over dal

YOGURT IN COOKING

Yogurt mellows the flavour of the spices in a dish and adds a creaminess and delicate tang. It must be added very carefully, however, as it curdles very easily. Add yogurt 15 ml (1 tbsp) at a time, stirring well after each addition, and do not add the next spoonful of yogurt until the yogurt is well blended. Avoid boiling sauces after yogurt has been added. (See also *Marinating*.)

SPECIAL EQUIPMENT

Very little special equipment is needed to cook Indian food successfully. The utensils and pots and pans you use everyday will be quite suitable. The following is a selection of cooking tools you would find in most Indian homes.

DEGCHI

This brass or aluminium cooking pot is used throughout India and is the universal cooking tool. It is like a saucepan without handles, has straight sides with a horizontal rim. The flat lid fits over the rim which is often sealed with a flour and water paste for dum cooking. Hot coals are placed on the lid to provide heat from above as well.

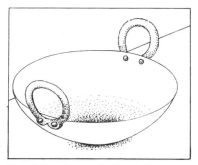

Traditional deep-frying dish

KARHAI

This is very similar in shape to a Chinese wok. It is used mainly for deep-frying and because of its

shape is very economical in its use of oil. A wok or deep-fat fryer makes a good substitute.

KATORI AND THALI

Katori are small metal bowls used for serving individual portions of food at Indian meals. A thali is a large circular tray used for rice, breads and pickles. The katori are usually placed just inside the rim of the thali. The dishes can be made of gold or silver, but are more commonly made of brass or stainless steel.

SEV-MAKER

A sev machine is used to make the popular snack food made from gram flour. The prepared dough is squeezed straight into the hot fat through small holes in interchangeable discs. Sev-makers can be bought from Indian grocery stores.

SPICE GRINDER

Spices were originally ground by hand using a grinding stone. An electric coffee grinder or small electric mill is excellent for this purpose and takes the effort out of grinding your own spices. Failing that, a pestle and mortar can be used. Remember to wipe out your coffee grinder with damp absorbent kitchen paper after each use or process a slice of bread into breadcrumbs to absorb the flavours. (See also page 141.)

TAVA

Breads such as chapatis, rotis and parathas are all cooked on this flat, heavy cast iron sheet. A griddle or heavy frying pan (not non-stick) is a good substitute.

Special Ingredients

This chapter concentrates on the special ingredients you are likely to need. You need not buy them all, but build up your stores of spices, herbs, pulses etc. as you go along—you may find you have many of them already.

COCONUT

Coconut is widely used in both sweet and savoury dishes, particularly those from Southern India.

HOW TO CHECK IF A COCONUT IS FRESH

1 Shake the coconut to check there is liquid inside. The more liquid, the fresher the coconut.

2 Examine the 'eyes' at one end of the nut. They should be intact and just yield to pressure from the thumb.

HOW TO OPEN A COCONUT

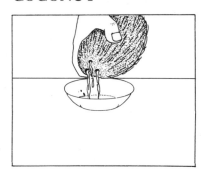

1 Pierce two of the 'eyes' of the nut with a screwdriver and drain out the liquid. This can be used for making coconut milk or as a drink.

2 Wrap the nut in a tea-towel and break it with a hammer. Remove the coconut flesh using a strong knife.

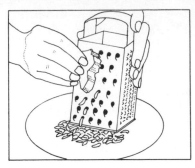

3 The flesh can now be grated, or sliced or used for making coconut milk.

COCONUT MILK

The coconut milk referred to in many recipes has nothing to do with the natural 'milk' or juice in the centre of the coconut, but is actually made using either fresh coconut or creamed coconut. In Indian and Southeast Asian dishes, it gives a subtle, creamy flavour and takes the harsh 'edge' off hot, fiery spices.

HOW TO MAKE COCONUT MILK USING A FRESH COCONUT

Makes about 100 ml (4 fl oz) thick coconut milk or 250 ml (9 fl oz) thin coconut milk.

1 Grate the flesh of 1 coconut into a bowl, add 125 ml (4 fl oz) coconut liquid or cold water and leave for 20 minutes.

2 Place a sieve over a bowl. Turn the soaked coconut into the sieve and press with the back of a spoon to extract as much liquid as possible. The resulting liquid will be thick coconut milk.

3 To make thin coconut milk, return the squeezed coconut to the bowl and add 150 ml ($\frac{1}{4}$ pint) coconut liquid or cold water. Leave to soak for 15 minutes.

4 Press again through the sieve. The resulting liquid will be thinner than before.

CREAMED COCONUT
This is sold in blocks in larger supermarkets, ethnic stores and delicatessens. It is convenient to use and less expensive than fresh coconut for making coconut milk.

COCONUT MILK USING CREAMED COCONUT
Makes 450 ml ($\frac{3}{4}$ pint) thick coconut milk or 600 ml (1 pint) thin coconut milk.

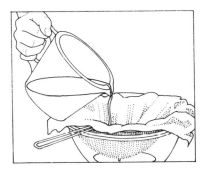

1 Break 198 g (7 oz) packet of creamed coconut into a bowl. Add 450 ml ($\frac{3}{4}$ pint) warm water. Stir until dissolved. This will make a thick milk. Strain through muslin or a fine sieve before use.

2 For a thinner milk, stir in an extra 150 ml ($\frac{1}{4}$ pint) water. Strain through muslin or a fine sieve before use.

FLOUR

Indian breads are almost always unleavened. They are made from flours ground from a range of different ingredients, all of which are available at Indian grocers, and some at health food shops. Apart from wheat, oats, barley and buckwheat, many dals are ground into flours. Channa dal, moong dal and masoor dal are traditionally ground by hand and used to make savoury pancakes such as dosas and for various savoury snacks and dumplings. Cornmeal is used to make the traditional bread of Punjab. Gram flour (also called besan) is widely used for many savoury dishes, as a base for batters and as an emulsifier when added to yogurt. Rice flour is used for savoury pancakes and in making sweet milk puddings. The traditional flour for making breads such as chapatis and parathas is called atta, which is a coarsely ground wholemeal flour. Roasted chick pea flour is added to dishes for its flavouring and thickening properties. Plain flour or *maida* is normally used for savoury dishes and for making pastry.

FOOD COLOURINGS

In India, food is often brightly coloured. The colour is mostly achieved with spices such as turmeric, paprika and saffron, but for a really dazzling effect, edible food colourings are used. Yellow is used for rice dishes, orange and red for tandoori food, and green for sweet dishes.

FRUIT AND VEGETABLES

AUBERGINES
These are grown in India and are used extensively in curries, fritters, sauces and are sometimes stuffed. They come in various shades from pink to purple, green and white.

BITTER GOURD
Known as *karela* in Indian, they look a little like courgettes with a knobbly surface. It must be carefully prepared to reduce the bitterness before being used in

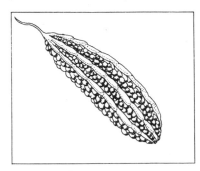

Bitter gourd

cooking. Cut the top off the gourd and rub the outside skin against the cut surface of the gourd. A kind of foam is created. Rinse the gourd and cut into slices.

GREEN BANANAS
These are always cooked before being eaten. They taste more mealy than the yellow banana and are used in a variety of dishes.

GUAVA
A fruit with a creamy yellow skin and pink flesh with small dark seeds. It has a delicate flavour.

LIMES
The juice of the lime is used mainly as a drink and to add a sour flavour to dishes. Limes are also made into a powerful pickle.

LOTUS SEEDS
They are dried and used in India to make a kind of popcorn.

MANGO

These fruit are much prized in India. The skin can vary from green, yellow to deep pink and the flesh has a similar texture to that of a peach, although more fibrous. Unripe mangoes are used to make pickles and chutneys.

OKRA or BHINDI

These are also called 'ladies fingers', because of their long tapering shape. They are green pods with white flesh and edible

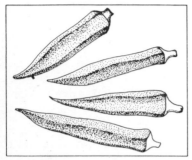

Okra, bhindi or 'ladies fingers'

seeds. Wipe them with a damp cloth and remove the stems before cooking.

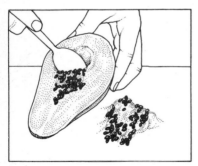

Remove papaya seeds before serving

PAPAYA

A delicious, soft-fleshed fruit with a green or deep yellow skin. It has delicately flavoured soft flesh which is orangey pink. Papaya is popular as a breakfast dish served with lemon juice.

GHEE

Ghee is clarified butter which is used extensively in Indian cooking, particularly in Northern India. It has a rich flavour and imparts a slightly nutty taste to the food in which it is cooked. Because it is so pure, it can be heated to high temperatures and is therefore suitable for both deep and shallow frying. There is a vegetarian ghee also available but it is considered far inferior in taste to true ghee. You can buy ghee in cans at Indian grocers and in packets at some good supermarkets and delicatessens. The packet ghee is solid and should be melted over a gentle heat, then cooled before measuring and using.

HOW TO MAKE GHEE

1 Melt 225 g (8 oz) unsalted butter gently in a heavy-based saucepan. Simmer until a thick froth appears.

2 Continue to simmer the butter for 10–20 minutes until the froth starts to separate from the clear golden liquid, and some of the sediment settles at the bottom. Keep checking the butter as it burns easily.

3 Remove from the heat and cool slightly. Line a sieve with muslin or absorbent kitchen paper. Place over a bowl and pour the ghee through, taking care not to disturb the sediment.

4 Leave to cool slightly, then transfer to a jar, cover and refrigerate for up to 3–4 weeks.

OILS

Generally speaking, where oil is called for in a recipe, corn or vegetable oil is fine for this purpose, and in recipes calling for ghee, either of these oils can be used as a substitute if ghee is unavailable. Sometimes, special oils are used to impart a particular flavour to a dish. The choice of oils used also varies greatly from one region to another.

COCONUT OIL

This oil comes from the inner white flesh of the coconut and is particularly popular in Southern and Western India. It is a colourless saturated fat with a mild flavour.

GROUNDNUT OIL

This comes from peanuts and is excellent for all cooking purposes. It is much used in Southern India and is prized for its light flavour and purity.

MUSTARD OIL

A pungent, deep golden oil extracted from mustard seeds. It is mainly used in the cooking of Bengal and Kashmir, and is a popular ingredient in pickles.

SESAME OIL

Indian sesame oil is a light colourless oil and should not be confused with the more commonly available Chinese sesame oil which is darker in colour and heavier. If you are unable to find the light sesame oil, use 1 part dark sesame oil to 3 parts vegetable oil. Sesame oil is used in Southern, Central and Western regions of India. It is used in small quantities, usually to fry spices before adding them to a dish.

DAL (PULSES)

Dal is the collective name given to the great variety of pulses, dried peas and lentils cooked in India. Dals are rich in protein and play a crucial role in the diets of many vegetarians. Pulses are sold either whole or split, and they are also ground into flour to make batters and pastes. One disadvantage of dals is that they can be a little indigestible, which is why certain spices known for their digestive qualities are often cooked with them. These include ajowan and asafoetida. Spices are also used to produce a wealth of different tastes using comparatively simple ingredients.

CHANNA DAL
These are the husked, split black chick pea. They are deep yellow in colour and similar to yellow split peas.

CHHOLE
Whole chick peas. These heart-shaped, beige coloured peas are available in most supermarkets.

KALE CHANNA
Like chick peas but darker and smaller.

LOBIA
Whole black-eyed beans.

MASOOR DAL
Whole masoor dal are called Saabat Masoor. These brown or pale green lentils are best soaked before cooking, unlike the split red lentils which can be boiled without soaking. Usually boiled with spices and sometimes other vegetables to form a thick sauce.

MOONG OR MUNG DAL
Whole moong beans are called Sabaat Mung. These small, yellow beans with green husks tend to be tough and are not soaked before cooking. After long simmering the skin will split and the bean becomes tender and mushy. Split

Moong dal with the skin left on is Mung Dal Chilke Wali. These should be soaked for at least an hour before cooking. Dhooli Hui Moong Dal are split with the skins removed. These little yellow beans need only brief soaking. Moong dal is also ground into flour.

RAJMA DAL
These are red kidney beans, with a mild nutty flavour, which are much used in North and Central India. They should be soaked overnight before cooking and then boiled hard for 10 minutes before continuing the cooking at a simmer until tender. This method is essential to rid the bean of a toxic enzyme it contains when raw.

SPROUTED DALS
These are whole beans which are sprouted. Most can be sprouted successfully at home. Simply wash the beans and spread them over a dish. Cover with warm water and leave in a dark place for 24 hours. Drain the beans, then rinse them twice and cover again with water. Return the dish to the dark place. Continue rinsing the beans twice daily for about 4 days.

TOOVAR OR ARHAR DAL
Round, yellowish split pea.

URAD DAL
Saabat Urad is the name of the whole black bean. These small black beans, about 0.5 cm ($\frac{1}{4}$ inch) long, require lengthy cooking to tenderise. Urad Dal Chilke Wali is the split dal with its skins left on. The dal forms a glutinous liquid to give it a creamy texture. Dhuli Hui Urad Dal is the split dal with the skins removed. This is often ground and used to make fritters. These beans are mostly used in their split form in the cooking of Punjab. Although similar in appearance, Urad Dal is not the same as the common American black bean and this should not be used as a substitute.

RICE

Rice is of prime importance in Indian cooking, and there are countless ways of cooking it. Rice dishes can be served as starters, main meals, accompaniments, snacks and even for breakfast. Ground rice is used to make batters and pancakes.

For every day cooking, long grain or patna rice is used, and in Indian cookery it should be dry and fluffy. For special occasions, basmati rice—the 'king of rice'—is used. Basmati rice is grown in India and Pakistan. The best quality basmati rice comes from the foot-hills of the Himalayas. It is a type of long grain rice but the grains are long and slender, with a delicate flavour all its own. Basmati rice must be cooked carefully and stirred just once at the beginning of the cooking to prevent the grains breaking up. When cooked, the grains bend slightly to become sickle shaped.

There are several ways to cook rice, and many schools of thought on the best way to achieve perfect results. Most cooks have their own favourite method of boiling ordinary long grain or patna rice, some using a large volume of water, others using the absorption method in which the rice is cooked in twice its own volume of water. If you have a foolproof method for cooking long grain rice, it is best to continue with it, but for cooking basmati rice, the instructions overleaf should be followed.

HOW TO COOK BASMATI RICE

1 First, pick over the rice to remove any stones. Put the rice in a sieve and rinse under cold running water until the water runs clear. Transfer the rice to a bowl and cover with plenty of cold water. Soak for 30 minutes.

2 Drain the rice well and leave to stand for 2 minutes. If the rice is to be fried before cooking, leave it to dry completely.

3 Put the rice in a heavy-based saucepan or flameproof casserole. Shake the pan to level the rice. Sprinkle with salt, allowing 2.5 ml ($\frac{1}{2}$ tsp) salt to each 225 g (8 oz) rice. Add cold water to cover the rice by about 2.5 cm (1 inch).

4 Bring the water gently to the boil. Reduce the heat to a simmer, then cover the pan tightly with a lid and cook very gently for 15 minutes. Do not lift the lid during the cooking time or valuable steam will escape.

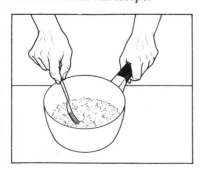

5 There is no need to rinse the cooked rice, simply fluff it up to separate the grains.

HERBS, SPICES AND FLAVOURINGS

The following alphabetical list covers the main herbs, spices and flavourings you are most likely to need for the recipes in this book.

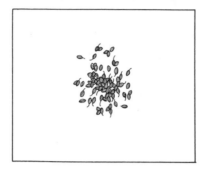

AJOWAN

Small, light brown slightly elongated seeds. Ajowan is similar in flavour to thyme, and a relative of caraway and cumin. Used to flavour food and for its digestive properties.

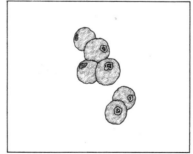

ALLSPICE

Also known as Jamaica pepper. The seeds of allspice are slightly larger than peppercorns and dark brown in colour. It has a delicate, spicy flavour with a hint of cloves, cinnamon and nutmeg.

ANISEED OR FENNEL SEEDS

These tiny tear-shaped seeds have a warm, sweet pungent flavour. Their taste and smell is similar to liquorice. It is used whole or ground, mainly in Bengali and Kashmiri-style dishes.

ASAFOETIDA

This pungent resin is used in Indian cooking as a digestive. It is not easy to find, though the ground form is more common than the solid block. Used very sparingly in pickles, fish and vegetable dishes.

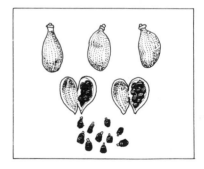

CARDAMOM

Cardamom pods are either green or black, the green ones having the finest flavour. The pods are added whole to dishes, or the black seeds inside extracted and used whole or ground. Cardamom seeds are an essential ingredient of garam masala. White cardamom pods are also available but are bleached and inferior in taste.

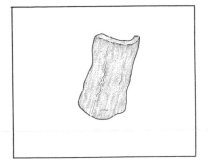

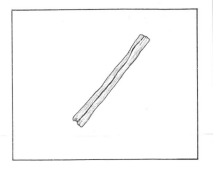

CASSIA

Cassia bark is a relative of cinnamon and has a strong cinnamon flavour. Pieces are added to many Indian dishes. It has a coarser appearance than true cinnamon quills or sticks.

CAYENNE

Cayenne pepper is ground from the pods and seeds of a hot, red variety of the capsicum family. It should be used sparingly as it is extremely hot and spicy.

CHAAT MASALA

This is a popular mixture of dry fried spices, much used in Indian cookery.

15 ml (1 tbsp) coriander seeds
15 ml (1 tbsp) cumin seeds
5 ml (1 tsp) black peppercorns
3 whole dried red chillies

1 Put all the spices in a small frying pan and dry fry until the seeds begin to colour slightly and pop and splutter. Remove from the heat.

2 Transfer the spices to a small electric mill or pestle and mortar and grind to a fine powder. Store in an airtight container.

CHILLIES

Small hot varieties of capsicum, chillies are either red or green. Fresh chillies are small and tapering with smooth shiny skin. The green chillies are unripe red chillies. The seeds have the most powerful flavour and some or all of these can be removed if it is flavour rather than heat that is required. Dried red chillies have a concentrated flavour and should be used in small quantities. Chilli powder varies in intensity from one brand to another, so check first before using.

HOW TO PREPARE CHILLIES

1 Slit the chilli down the length and remove all or some of the seeds with the point of a knife.

2 Slice finely or chop as required. Always wash your hands thoroughly immediately after handling chillies.

CINNAMON

Cinnamon is the bark of a tree which grows in tropical forests. It is sold in sticks or ground. It has a highly aromatic flavour.

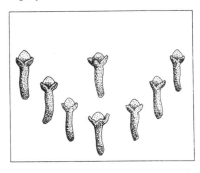

CLOVES

These are nearly always used whole in Indian cooking to add an aromatic flavour. They are an essential ingredient of garam masala (see page 140).

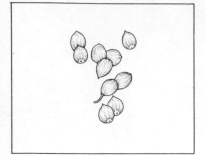

CORIANDER

The seeds of the coriander are used as a spice and the leaves as a herb. The round light brown seeds have a fresh spicy flavour and can be used whole or ground in many Indian dishes. They are sometimes dry fried before being ground to bring out their full flavour. Coriander leaves are a favourite Indian herb and are often chopped and stirred into dishes at the end of the cooking time to retain flavour.

TO STORE FRESH CORIANDER LEAVES

1 Place the roots of the bunch into a container of water, such as a jam jar or jug. The leaves should not be in the water.

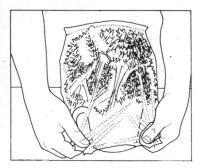

2 Place a large polythene bag over the coriander and its container to completely enclose it.

3 Place in the refrigerator or in a cool place. The coriander will last for 2–3 weeks. Remove any yellowing leaves before use.

CUMIN

This comes in two varieties. An ingredient of garam masala, cumin is used whole or ground.

CURRY LEAVES

Thin dark green leaves with the flavour of curry powder. They are mainly used in South and West Indian cooking. Lightly frying the leaves in hot oil brings out their flavour.

CURRY POWDER

For authentic Indian dishes, do not buy commercial brands of curry powder; recipes in this book specify individual spices. If you are short of time when making a curry, however, you may find it useful to have your own home-made 'curry powder' to hand.

CURRY POWDER

Makes 300 g (20 tbsp)

30 ml (2 tbsp) cumin seeds
30 ml (2 tbsp) fenugreek seeds
7.5 ml (1½ tsp) mustard seeds
15 ml (1 tbsp) black peppercorns
120 ml (8 tbsp) coriander seeds
15 ml (1 tbsp) poppy seeds
15 ml (1 tbsp) ground ginger
5 ml (1 tsp) chilli powder
60 ml (4 tbsp) turmeric

1 Finely grind all the spices in a small electric mill or with a pestle and mortar.

2 Store in an airtight container. Curry powder will keep for up to 3 months.

DHANIA ZEERA

A frequently used spice mixture, which is simple to make.

100 g (4 oz) coriander seeds
25 g (1 oz) cumin seeds
15 g (½ oz) whole dried red chillies

1 Finely grind all the spices in a small electric mill or with a pestle and mortar to a fine powder. Store in an airtight container.

FENUGREEK

Fenugreek seeds are small, mustard coloured rectangular seeds. They are usually used whole and have a rather bitter, pungent flavour. Fenugreek leaves are used as a herb or a vegetable.

GARAM MASALA

Recipes for garam masala, which literally translated means 'hot spices', vary greatly, but usually contain cardamoms, cinnamon, cumin, cloves, pepper and nutmeg. The mixture is used sparingly, and is often added towards the end of the cooking time, or sprinkled over cooked dishes before being brought to the table. Garam masala should be made in small quantities as the flavour does not stay fresh long.

GARAM MASALA

Makes about 45 ml (3 tbsp)

15 ml (1 tbsp) cardamom seeds
5 cm (2 inch) piece of cassia bark
5 ml (1 tsp) cumin seeds, preferably black
5 ml (1 tsp) whole cloves
5 ml (1 tsp) black peppercorns
⅓ nutmeg, grated

1 Finely grind all the spices in a small electric mill or with a pestle and mortar. Store in an airtight container for up to 3 weeks.

GARLIC
Garlic is a member of the onion family and is considered to have medicinal properties. Fresh crushed garlic is added to many Indian dishes.

GINGER
Fresh ginger comes from the root-like stems of a tropical plant. When buying fresh root ginger, check that the skin is unwrinkled and that the flesh feels firm. The skin is peeled away before use, then the ginger can be chopped, sliced, grated or made into a paste. When grating ginger, use the finest blade. Ground ginger is rarely used in Indian cookery.

KALONGI
Small tear-shaped hard black seeds; much used in making Indian breads and vegetable dishes, as well as for pickling. Sometimes called onion seeds.

KEWRA WATER
This is used to impart a flowery perfume to a variety of dishes, particularly Indian sweets, such as ice cream and puddings.

MINT
Mint adds flavour to many curries and fresh mint chutney is a favourite accompaniment to a biryani meal, or as a dipping sauce for samosas.

MUSTARD SEEDS
Black, brown and white mustard seeds are available. The mustard seeds used in Indian cooking are small and reddish-brown in colour. Frying the seeds in hot oil extracts their delicious flavour.

POPPY SEEDS
White poppy seeds are used in Indian curries mainly for thickening. They are often ground before being added to dishes. Black poppy seeds are no substitute as they have a quite different flavour.

ROSE WATER
Rose water is much used in making Indian sweets. It is a diluted essence extracted from rose petals. Use carefully as it should add a subtle flavour to the food. Rose water is available in Indian food stores and chemists.

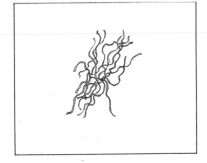

SAFFRON
The most expensive spice in the world, saffron comes from the dried stamens of the saffron crocus. The thread-like strands are dark orange and have a distinctive perfume. Saffron strands are soaked in warm liquid before use to extract their colour and flavour. Powdered saffron is also available. Saffron is mostly used in Northern Indian dishes.

SESAME SEEDS
These beige seeds have a mildly nutty flavour. They are often roasted to bring out their flavour.

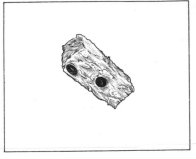

TAMARIND
This is the semi-dried fruit of the tamarind tree. The fruit is soaked in water before use and the sour liquid used to flavour curries, chutneys and sauces.

TAMARIND JUICE
Makes about 75 ml (5 tbsp)

15 ml (1 tbsp) dried tamarind pulp

60 ml (4 tbsp) warm water

1 Soak the dried pulp in the warm water for 15 minutes. Strain the liquid through a sieve, pressing down hard with a wooden spoon to extract as much of the pulp as possible.

2 Discard the pulp left in the sieve and use the juice according to the recipe.

TURMERIC
Ground turmeric is bright yellow in colour and has a mild, slightly musty flavour. It is used mainly as a colouring ingredient in dishes.

GRINDING YOUR OWN SPICES
Freshly ground spices are far superior in flavour to ready ground ones. Small quantities of spices can be ground with a pestle and mortar or with a rolling pin. Grind larger quantities in an electric coffee grinder or small electric mill.

DRY FRYING SPICES
Dry frying (sometimes also referred to as 'dry roasting' or 'roasting') mellows the flavour of spices. The spices can be fried singly or in mixtures. If mixing the spices, put the hardest ones, such as fenugreek, into the pan first, then add the softer ones such as cumin and coriander. Heat a heavy frying pan (not non-stick) over moderate heat. Add the spices and stir them all the time until they are evenly browned. Tip them out of the pan, cool slightly, then grind them if required.

Breads

One of the many different types of Indian breads is always served at an Indian meal. These breads are used to scoop up the curries; nan and chapatis being the best for this purpose. Poppadoms (page 18) are crispy and often used as an appetiser with predinner drinks. Mainly unleavened, Indian breads are usually fairly bland to complement the spicy food. However some breads have interesting vegetable and spice stuffings.

PURIS
(DEEP-FRIED UNLEAVENED WHOLEMEAL BREAD)
Makes 12

225 g (8 oz) plain wholemeal flour
pinch of salt
30 ml (2 tbsp) ghee or vegetable oil
vegetable oil, for deep-frying

1 Put the flour and salt in a bowl. Sprinkle the ghee over the top. Gradually mix in 150–200 ml (5–7 fl oz) water to form a stiff dough.

2 Turn on to a lightly floured surface and knead thoroughly for 6–8 minutes until smooth and elastic.

3 Return the dough to the bowl, cover with a damp clean cloth and leave to rest for 15 minutes.

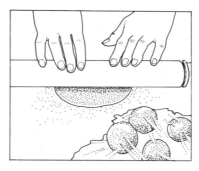

4 Divide the dough into 12 and roll each piece into a small ball. On a lightly floured surface, roll out one ball to a round about 12.5 cm (5 inches) in diameter. Keep the remaining balls covered. If you have the space, roll out the remaining puris in the same way and, as you proceed, cover with cling film.

5 Heat about 5 cm (2 inches) of oil in a small, deep frying pan until very hot.

6 Carefully slide a puri into the hot fat. Using the back of a slotted spoon, press the puri into the oil and cook over low heat for about 10 seconds. It will begin to puff up immediately. Turn the puri over and, still pressing with the spoon, fry until golden brown and puffed up.

7 Drain the puri on absorbent kitchen paper. Keep hot. Continue cooking the remaining puris in the same way.

NAN
(FLAT LEAVENED WHITE BREAD)
This flat, tear-drop shaped bread is traditionally baked on the side of a tandoor oven.

Makes 6

15 g ($\frac{1}{2}$ oz) fresh yeast or 7.5 ml (1$\frac{1}{2}$ tsp) dried
200 ml (7 fl oz) tepid milk
450 g (1 lb) plain white flour
5 ml (1 tsp) baking powder
2.5 ml ($\frac{1}{2}$ tsp) salt
10 ml (2 tsp) caster sugar
1 egg, beaten
30 ml (2 tbsp) vegetable oil
60 ml (4 tbsp) natural yogurt

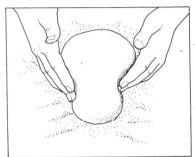

BHATURA
(DEEP-FRIED BREAD)
Makes 6–8

60 ml (4 tbsp) natural yogurt
175 g (6 oz) plain flour
2.5 ml ($\frac{1}{2}$ tsp) salt
2.5 ml ($\frac{1}{2}$ tsp) sugar
2.5 ml ($\frac{1}{2}$ tsp) bicarbonate of soda
5 ml (1 tsp) ghee or butter, softened
vegetable oil, for deep-frying

1 Blend the fresh yeast and 150 ml ($\frac{1}{4}$ pint) of the milk together. If using dried yeast, sprinkle it into 150 ml ($\frac{1}{4}$ pint) of the milk and leave in a warm place for 15 minutes until frothy.

5 Knead the dough on a lightly floured surface for 2–3 minutes, then divide into 6 equal pieces. Roll out each piece on a lightly floured surface and shape into a large tear-drop about 25 cm (10 inches) long.

1 Warm the yogurt slightly by putting it into a small bowl and standing the bowl in a basin of hot water. Leave for 5 minutes to warm through.

6 Place a nan on a baking sheet and put under a preheated hot grill. Cook for 1½–2 minutes on each side until golden brown and puffy. Cook the remaining nan in the same way. Serve warm.

2 Sift the flour into a bowl with the salt, sugar and bicarbonate of soda. Make a well in the centre and add the yogurt and about 60 ml (4 tbsp) water. Mix to a soft smooth dough.

2 Sift the flour, baking powder and salt into a large bowl. Make a well in the centre and stir in the sugar, egg, oil and yogurt.

— VARIATION —

Peshawari Nan *(Nan with sultanas and almonds)*

Follow the recipe above to the beginning of step 5. To make the filling, mix together 175 g (6 oz) sultanas, 175 g (6 oz) ground almonds and 90 ml (6 tbsp) ghee. Knead the dough on a lightly floured surface and divide into 6 equal pieces. Roll out into a round about 15 cm (6 inches) in diameter. Spoon the filling into the centre of the Nan and fold over the dough to completely enclose the filling. Press the edges well together to seal. Roll out each piece on a lightly floured surface and shape into a large tear-drop about 25 cm (10 inches) long. Cook as in step 6 of the recipe above.

3 Add the yeast liquid and mix well to a soft dough, adding more milk if necessary. Turn the dough on to a lightly floured surface and knead well for 10 minutes until smooth and elastic.

3 Tip out of the bowl and knead for 2–3 minutes until smooth and elastic. Work in the ghee and knead once more until smooth. Place in a bowl, cover with cling film and leave to rise for 3 hours.

4 Divide into 6–8 even-sized pieces and roll into balls. Keep these covered with cling film to prevent them drying out. On a floured surface, roll each ball into a 10 cm (4 inch) round, cover with cling film.

4 Place the dough in a bowl, cover with a cloth and leave to rise in a warm place for about 1 hour until doubled in size.

5 Heat oil in a deep-fat fryer to 150°C (300°F) and deep-fry each one until puffed and golden. Drain on absorbent kitchen paper and serve immediately.

CHAPATIS
(UNLEAVENED WHOLEMEAL BREAD)
Makes 6

225 g (8 oz) plain wholemeal flour
ghee or melted butter, for
brushing

1 Put the flour in a bowl and gradually mix in 150–200 ml (5–7 fl oz) water to form a stiff dough.

2 Turn on to a lightly floured surface and, with floured hands, knead thoroughly for 6–8 minutes until smooth and elastic.

3 Return the dough to the bowl, cover with a damp clean cloth and leave to rest for 15 minutes.

4 Heat a tava (flat Indian frying pan), heavy frying pan or griddle over a low flame until really hot. Meanwhile, divide the dough into 6 pieces. With floured hands, take a piece of dough and shape into a smooth ball.

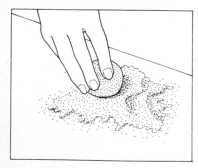

5 Dip the ball of dough in flour to coat, then roll out on a floured surface to a round about 18 cm (7 inches) in diameter.

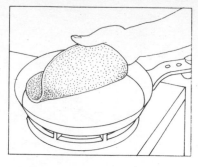

6 Slap the chapati on to the hot pan. Cook over a low flame and as soon as brown specks appear on the underside, turn it over and repeat on the other side.

7 Turn the chapati over again and, with a clean tea towel, press down the edges of the chapati to circulate the steam and make the chapati puff up. Cook until the underside is golden brown, then cook the other side in the same way.

8 Brush the chapati with ghee or melted butter. Serve at once or keep warm wrapped in foil. Continue cooking the remaining chapatis in the same way.

PARATHAS
(SHALLOW-FRIED UNLEAVENED WHOLEMEAL BREAD)
Parathas can be made in any combination of the shapes below.
Makes 8

225 g (8 oz) plain wholemeal flour
ghee or melted butter,
for brushing

1 Make the dough as for chapatis (see left) and leave to rest as in step 3.

2 Divide the dough into 8 pieces. With floured hands, take a piece of dough and shape into a smooth ball. Dip in flour to coat, then roll out on a floured surface into 1 of the shapes below.

Triangular Parathas

1 Roll out the piece of dough to a round about 12.5 cm (5 inches) in diameter. Brush a little melted ghee on top.

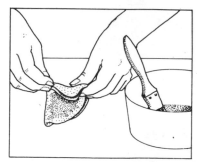

2 Fold the round in half, brush the top with ghee and fold in half again to make a triangle.

3 Press the layers together and, using a little extra flour, roll out thinly into a large triangle, the sides measuring about 18 cm (7 inches). Cover with a damp clean cloth and roll out the remaining dough to make 8 parathas altogether.

Round Parathas

1 Roll out the piece of dough to a round about 18 cm (7 inches) in diameter. Brush a little melted ghee on top.

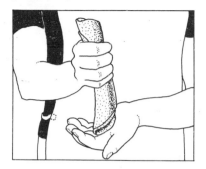

2 Roll the round into a tube shape. Hold the tube upright and place 1 end in the centre of your hand.

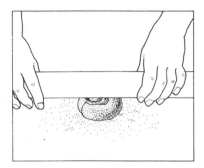

3 Wind the rest of the roll carefully around the centre point to form a disc. Press lightly together and, using a little extra flour, roll out thinly into a round about 18 cm (7 inches) in diameter. Cover with a damp clean cloth and roll out the remaining dough to make 8 parathas altogether.

Square Parathas

1 Roll out the piece of dough to a round about 12.5 cm (5 inches) in diameter. Brush a little melted ghee on top.

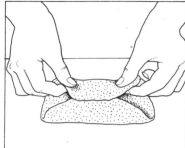

2 Fold one side of the round into the centre and fold in the opposite side to meet the first, forming a rectangle.

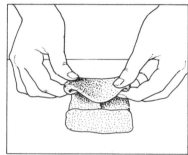

3 Brush the top with ghee and repeat the folding to form a square. Using a little extra flour, roll out thinly into a square about 18 cm (7 inches). Cover with a damp clean cloth and roll out the remaining dough to make 8 parathas altogether.

4 Heat a tava (flat Indian frying pan), heavy frying pan or griddle over a low flame until really hot. Place 1 paratha in the pan and cook over a low flame until small bubbles appear on the surface.

5 Turn the paratha over and brush the top with melted ghee. Cook until the underside is golden brown, then turn again and brush with more ghee.

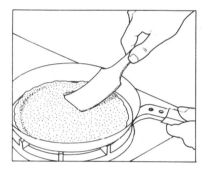

6 Press down the edges of the paratha with a spatula to ensure even cooking and cook the other side until golden brown.

7 Brush with more ghee and serve at once or keep warm wrapped in foil. Continue cooking the remaining parathas in the same way.

AJOWAN PARATHAS

Makes 12

350 g (12 oz) plain wholemeal flour
15 ml (1 tbsp) ajowan seeds
5 ml (1 tsp) salt
3.75 ml (¾ tsp) chilli powder
120 ml (8 tbsp) ghee or melted butter

1 Put the flour, ajowan seeds, salt and chilli powder in a bowl and mix well together. Add about 300 ml (½ pint) cold water and bind to a soft pliable dough — it may be slightly sticky.

2 Turn the dough on to a lightly floured surface and knead with floured hands for 6–8 minutes, using a little flour if necessary, until smooth and elastic. Cover the dough with a damp clean cloth and leave to rest for about 15 minutes.

3 Divide the dough into 12 pieces. Take a piece of dough and shape into a smooth ball. Roll out on a lightly floured surface into a round about 15 cm (6 inches) in diameter.

4 Brush a little ghee over the paratha, then roll into a tube shape (see step 2 of Round Parathas, page 145). Hold the tube upright and place 1 end in the centre of your hand.

5 Wind the rest of the roll carefully around the centre point to form a disc (see step 3 of Round Parathas, page 145).

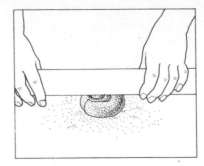

6 Press lightly together and roll out on a floured surface to a round about 15 cm (6 inches) in diameter. Cover with a damp clean cloth and roll out the remaining dough to make 12 parathas altogether.

7 Put a tava, heavy frying pan or griddle over a low heat until really hot. Place 1 paratha in the pan and cook over low heat until small bubbles appear on the surface.

8 Turn the paratha over and brush the top with melted ghee. Cook for about 30 seconds until golden brown.

9 Turn the paratha again and brush with more ghee. Press down the edges of the paratha with a spatula to ensure even cooking and cook the other side until golden brown.

10 Brush with more ghee and serve at once or keep warm wrapped in foil while cooking the remainder.

SAG PARATHAS
(SPINACH STUFFED PARATHAS)

Makes 12

450 g (1 lb) plain wholemeal flour
salt
175 g (6 oz) unsalted cashew nuts
105 ml (7 tbsp) ghee or vegetable oil
3.75 ml (¾ tsp) chilli powder
7.5 ml (1½ tsp) cumin seeds
450 g (1 lb) frozen spinach, thawed and drained

1 Put the flour in a bowl, add a good pinch of salt and mix together. Bind to a soft dough with about 350 ml (12 fl oz) cold water.

2 Turn the dough on to a lightly floured surface and knead for 6–8 minutes until smooth and elastic. Cover the dough with a damp clean cloth and leave to rest for about 15 minutes.

3 Meanwhile, chop the nuts quite finely. Heat 45 ml (3 tbsp) ghee in a small frying pan, add the nuts and chilli powder and fry gently for 2–3 minutes, stirring frequently, until the nuts just begin to colour.

4 Remove the pan from the heat and stir in the cumin seeds and a little salt. Turn out into a bowl, leave to cool slightly, then stir in the spinach.

5 Divide the dough into 12 pieces. With floured hands, take a piece of dough and roll out to a round about 12.5 cm (5 inches) in diameter.

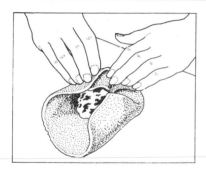

6 Spoon the filling into the centre of the paratha and fold over the dough to completely enclose the filling. Press the edges well together to seal.

7 On a well floured surface and using a floured rolling pin, roll out the filled dough round to a 15 cm (6 inch) circle. Cover with a damp clean cloth and roll out the remaining dough to make 12 stuffed parathas.

8 Put a tava (flat Indian frying pan), heavy frying pan or griddle over a low heat until really hot. Place 1 paratha in the pan and cook over low heat until small bubbles appear on the surface.

9 Turn the paratha over and brush the top with melted ghee. Cook until the underside is golden brown, then turn again and brush with more ghee.

10 Press down the edges of the paratha with a spatula to ensure even cooking and cook the second side until golden brown.

11 Brush with more ghee and serve at once or keep warm wrapped in foil. Continue cooking the remaining parathas in the same way.

DOSAS
(FRIED RICE AND LENTIL PANCAKE)

Dosas are a type of bread made from a pancake batter, and eaten with chutneys or relishes.

Makes 4

100 g (4 oz) basmati rice
100 g (4 oz) masoor dal (page 137)
5 ml (1 tsp) salt
45 ml (3 tbsp) ghee or vegetable oil

1 Wash the rice thoroughly, put in a bowl and leave to soak in plenty of cold water for about 1 hour. Wash and soak the dal separately.

2 Drain the rice and put in a blender or food processor. Add 90 ml (6 tbsp) water and blend until finely ground and like a batter. Transfer to a bowl.

3 Drain and blend the dal in the same way, adding 90 ml (6 tbsp) water. Add the dal to the rice with the salt and stir well.

4 Cover the bowl with a damp clean cloth and leave at room temperature for about 12 hours, or overnight.

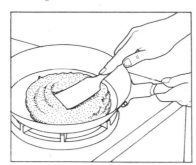

5 When ready to cook, heat 2.5 ml ($\frac{1}{2}$ tsp) of the ghee in a heavy frying pan. Pour in one-quarter of the batter and spread it evenly into a flat round about 18 cm (7 inches) in diameter.

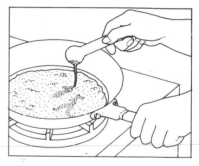

6 Fry for about 2–3 minutes until bubbles begin to form on the surface. Drizzle 2.5 ml ($\frac{1}{2}$ tsp) ghee over the top, then turn the pancake over with a spatula. Cook for a further 2 minutes until golden brown.

7 Transfer the dosa to a warmed serving dish and cover with a clean tea-towel to keep warm while cooking the remaining dosas in the same way. Serve warm.

——— VARIATIONS ———

The following flavourings can be added to the batter before frying: 1 skinned and finely chopped onion, 45 ml (3 tbsp) finely chopped fresh coriander, or 1 seeded and finely chopped green chilli.

Accompani-ments

Chutneys, relishes and salads are popular accompaniments to Indian meals. Which chutney or relish to serve is personal taste, however they are particularly good with drier dishes, such as dry curries, deep-fried foods and predinner snacks. Some chutneys and relishes are uncooked and will keep for a few days only, while others are cooked and need to mature first, but these have much longer keeping properties. A raita is a refreshing accompaniment to an Indian spread — the favourite combination is yogurt with cucumber but other vegetables work equally well. They help to cool down a spicy mixture, whilst salads stimulate digestive juices and increase appetite.

TAMATAR AUR DIAZ KI CHUTNEY
(TOMATO AND ONION CHUTNEY)

Makes about 2.3 kg (5 lb)

15 ml (1 tbsp) mustard seeds

900 g (2 lb) tomatoes, skinned and roughly chopped

450 g (1 lb) onions, skinned and chopped

1 garlic clove, skinned and chopped

900 g (2 lb) cooking apples, peeled, cored and sliced

225 g (8 oz) raisins

350 g (12 oz) granulated sugar

25 ml (5 tsp) curry powder (see page 140)

5 ml (1 tsp) cayenne pepper

20 ml (4 tsp) salt

900 ml (1½ pints) malt vinegar

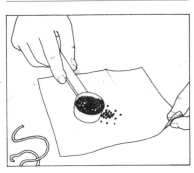

1 Put the mustard seeds in a piece of muslin or cheesecloth and tie securely with a long piece of string.

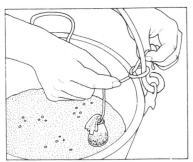

2 Put all the ingredients in a preserving pan with the muslin bag. Heat gently, stirring, until the sugar has dissolved.

3 Bring to the boil, then simmer gently, stirring occasionally, for about 3 hours until no excess liquid remains and the chutney is thick. Remove the muslin bag.

4 Spoon the chutney into pre-heated jars and cover at once with airtight, vinegar-proof tops.

5 Store in a cool, dry, dark place for 2–3 months to mature, before eating.

KHAJOOR AUR SANTRE KI CHUTNEY
(DATE AND ORANGE CHUTNEY)

Makes about 3.2 kg (7 lb)

450 g (1 lb) oranges

700 g (1½ lb) dates, stoned

450 g (1 lb) onions, skinned

225 g (8 oz) raisins

700 g (1½ lb) granulated sugar

30 ml (2 tbsp) salt

1.25 ml (¼ tsp) cayenne

1.4 litres (2½ pints) malt vinegar

1 Finely grate the rind of the oranges. Peel off the pith and slice the oranges, discarding all the pips.

2 Put the orange rind and slices and all the remaining ingredients in a preserving pan. Heat gently, stirring, until the sugar has dissolved. Bring to the boil, then simmer gently, stirring occasionally, for about 1 hour until no excess liquid remains and the chutney is thick.

3 Spoon the chutney into pre-heated jars and cover at once with airtight, vinegar-proof tops.

4 Store in a cool, dry, dark place for 2–3 months to mature, before eating.

PEACH CHUTNEY

Makes about 1.1 kg (2½ lb)

1 small piece of fresh root ginger, bruised

6 ripe peaches, skinned, stoned and sliced

100 g (4 oz) sultanas

2 large onions, skinned and finely chopped

15 ml (1 tbsp) salt

350 g (12 oz) granulated sugar

300 ml (½ pint) malt vinegar

15 ml (1 tbsp) mustard seeds

finely grated rind and juice of 1 lemon

1 Put the ginger in a piece of muslin or cheesecloth and tie securely with a long piece of string.

2 Put all the ingredients in a preserving pan with the muslin bag. Heat gently, stirring, until the sugar has dissolved.

3 Bring to the boil, then simmer gently, stirring occasionally, for about 1¾ hours, until no excess liquid remains and the chutney is thick. Remove the muslin bag.

4 Spoon the chutney into pre-heated jars and cover at once with airtight, vinegar-proof tops.

5 Store in a cool, dry, dark place for 2–3 months to mature, before eating.

AAM KI CHUTNEY
(MANGO CHUTNEY)

Makes about 2 kg (4½ lb)

1.8 kg (4 lb) unripe, green mangoes, peeled, sliced and stoned

225 g (8 oz) cooking apples, peeled, cored and chopped

225 g (8 oz) onions, skinned and chopped

100 g (4 oz) raisins

600 ml (1 pint) distilled malt vinegar

350 g (12 oz) granulated sugar

15 ml (1 tbsp) ground ginger

3 garlic cloves, skinned and crushed

5 ml (1 tsp) grated nutmeg

2.5 ml (½ tsp) salt

1 Put all the ingredients in a preserving pan. Heat gently, stirring, until the sugar has dissolved.

2 Bring to the boil, then simmer gently, stirring occasionally, for about 1½ hours until no excess liquid remains and the chutney is thick.

3 Spoon the mango chutney into preheated jars and cover at once with airtight, vinegar-proof tops.

4 Store in a cool, dry dark place for 2–3 months to mature, before eating.

NEEBU KA ACHAR
(LIME PICKLE)

Makes 450 g (1 lb)

450 g (1 lb) limes

45 ml (3 tbsp) salt

5 ml (1 tsp) turmeric

7.5 ml (1½ tsp) chilli powder

10 ml (2 tsp) garam masala (page 140)

1 Cut the fruit into small pieces, remove any pips and catch any juice in a bowl.

2 Mix the fruit pieces and juice with the salt, turmeric, chilli powder and garam masala.

3 Put into a large screw-topped jar and keep in a warm cupboard for about a week, giving it a good shake each day. The pickle is ready when the skins are tender. Store well covered in a cool, dry, dark place for up to 1 year.

PUDEENE KI CHUTNEY
(MINT CHUTNEY)

Fills a 350 g (12 oz) jar

50 g (2 oz) fresh mint leaves

60 ml (4 tbsp) fresh coriander leaves

1 medium onion, skinned

juice of ½–1 lemon

2.5 ml (½ tsp) sugar

2.5 ml (½ tsp) salt

1 Wash the mint and coriander leaves and dry thoroughly with absorbent kitchen paper.

2 Work the onion in a blender or food processor with a little lemon juice until minced.

3 Add the mint and coriander, sugar, salt and remaining lemon juice and blend to form a smooth paste.

4 Turn into a bowl, cover tightly and chill for about 1 hour before serving. Store for up to 2–3 days in the refrigerator.

CACHUMBER
(TOMATO, ONION AND CORIANDER RELISH)

Serves 4–6

225 g (8 oz) tomatoes
1 medium onion, skinned
1 green chilli, seeded
30 ml (2 tbsp) chopped fresh
   coriander leaves
15 ml (1 tbsp) lemon juice
salt and freshly ground pepper

1 Finely chop the tomatoes, onion and chilli and put in a salad bowl.

2 Add the coriander and lemon juice with salt and pepper to taste. Toss the ingredients well together.

3 Cover tightly and chill for about 1 hour before serving. The relish can be stored for up to 1–2 days in the refrigerator.

PIAZ KA IACCHA
(FRESH ONION RELISH)

Serves 4

1 medium onion, skinned
juice of 1 lemon
2.5 ml (½ tsp) paprika
salt and freshly ground pepper

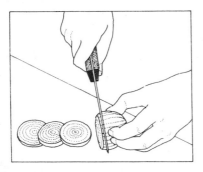

1 Cut the onion crossways into very, very thin rings. Put in a bowl and add the remaining ingredients, with salt and pepper to taste.

2 Toss together then cover tightly and leave to marinate for about 1 hour.

3 Chill for about 1 hour before serving. The relish can be stored for up to 1–2 days in the refrigerator.

HARI MIRCH KA ACHAR
(GREEN CHILLI PICKLE)

Makes 450 ml (¾ pint)

225 g (8 oz) fresh green chillies
300 ml (½ pint) vegetable oil
15 ml (1 tbsp) paprika
5 ml (1 tsp) turmeric
15 ml (1 tbsp) fennel seeds
15 ml (1 tbsp) mustard seeds
30 ml (2 tbsp) salt

1 Cut the chillies in half lengthways, remove the seeds and put into a clean, dry jar.

2 Heat the oil very slightly until just warm and add all the spices and salt. Stir well and leave to cool for 10 minutes.

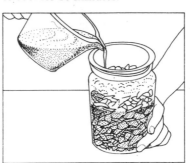

3 Pour the oil over the chillies and mix well. Cover the jar with muslin and leave in a warm place for 2–3 days, stirring the contents from time to time.

4 Remove the muslin and replace with a lid. Leave the pickle to mature in a cool place for at least 1 week before eating.

GARAM CHUTNEY
(HOT INDIAN CHUTNEY)

Makes about 2 kg (4½ lb)

700 g (1½ lb) cooking apples,
   peeled, cored and sliced
450 g (1 lb) onions, skinned and
   finely chopped
700 g (1½ lb) soft brown sugar
1.4 litres (2½ pints) malt vinegar
450 g (1 lb) seedless raisins,
   chopped
4 garlic cloves, skinned and
   crushed
20 ml (4 tsp) salt
30 ml (2 tbsp) ground ginger
45 ml (3 tbsp) mustard seeds
30 ml (2 tbsp) paprika
15 ml (1 tbsp) coriander seeds,
   crushed

1 Place all the ingredients in a large saucepan and bring to the boil. Simmer gently for about 3 hours, stirring occasionally, until no excess liquid remains.

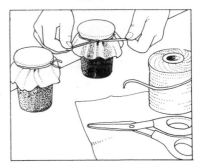

2 Spoon the chutney into pre-heated jars and cover at once with airtight, vinegar-proof tops.

3 Store in a cool, dry, dark place for 2–3 months to allow the flavours to mature.

KELAY KI CHUTNEY
(BANANA CHUTNEY)

Makes about 1.6 kg (3½ lb)

900 g (2 lb) bananas, peeled and sliced

100 g (4 oz) seedless raisins

100 g (4 oz) stoned dates, chopped

450 g (1 lb) cooking apples, peeled, cored and roughly chopped

100 g (4 oz) onions, skinned and chopped

5 ml (1 tsp) salt

175 g (6 oz) demerara sugar

15 ml (1 tbsp) ground ginger

2.5 ml (½ tsp) cayenne

300 ml (½ pint) distilled vinegar

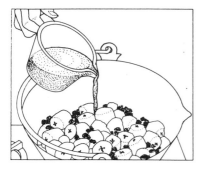

1 Place the prepared fruit and onions in a preserving pan and sprinkle with the salt, sugar and spices. Pour in the vinegar and bring gently to the boil. Simmer gently, stirring occasionally, for about 1 hour until no excess liquid remains and the mixture is soft and pulpy.

2 Spoon the chutney into pre-heated jars and cover at once with airtight and vinegar-proof tops.

3 Store in a cool, dry, dark place for 2–3 months to mature, before eating.

TAJE GAJJAR KI CHUTNEY
(FRESH CARROT CHUTNEY)

Makes 450 g (1 lb)

450 g (1 lb) carrots, peeled

1 small onion, skinned

45 ml (3 tbsp) chopped fresh mint

2.5 cm (1 inch) piece of fresh root ginger, peeled and finely chopped

7.5 ml (1½ tsp) salt

60 ml (4 tbsp) lemon or lime juice

1 Grate the carrot and onion finely and mix together with the mint, ginger and salt.

2 Add enough lemon or lime juice to moisten. Cover and refrigerate until required. This chutney will keep in the refrigerator for 2–3 days.

TAJE AAM KI CHUTNEY
(FRESH MANGO CHUTNEY)

Makes about 225 g (½ lb)

1 large ripe mango

1 fresh green chilli, seeded

juice of 1 lime

1.25 ml (¼ tsp) cayenne

2.5 ml (½ tsp) salt

1 Slice the mango in half length-ways through to the stone. Cut all the way round then, keeping the flat side of the knife against the stone, saw the mango flesh free from the stone. Repeat with the other side.

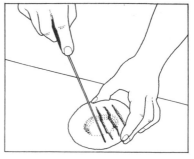

2 Using the point of a knife, make 5 or 6 diagonal cuts through the flesh, but not through the skin. Then make another 5 or 6 cuts at right angles to the first set, so that you have a diamond pattern in the flesh.

3 Turn the skin inside out so that the cubes of flesh stand up, then cut these off with the knife and place in a bowl.

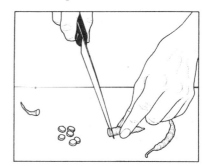

4 Cut the chilli into fine rings and mix with the mango cubes, lime juice, cayenne and salt. Chill for 1 hour before serving. This will only keep for up to 2 days in the refrigerator.

TAJEE DHANI YA KI CHUTNEY
(FRESH CORIANDER CHUTNEY)

Makes 300 ml (½ pint)

100 g (4 oz) fresh coriander, washed and dried

1 medium onion, skinned and roughly chopped

2 fresh green chillies, seeded

2.5 cm (1 inch) piece of fresh root ginger, peeled

5 ml (1 tsp) salt

30 ml (2 tbsp) lemon or lime juice

15 ml (1 tbsp) desiccated coconut

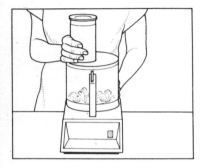

1 Put all the ingredients in a blender or food processor and work until smooth.

2 Transfer to a glass or plastic bowl, cover and chill in the refrigerator for up to 1 week.

BHUNI HUI PIAZ
(CRISP BROWNED ONIONS)

Makes enough to fill a 200 g (7 oz) jar

2 medium onions, skinned

vegetable oil, for frying

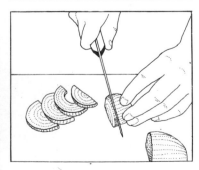

1 Cut the onions in half lengthways, then cut into thin slices.

2 Heat about 1 cm (½ inch) oil in a frying pan. When hot, add the onions and fry until golden brown, stirring all the time.

3 Remove the onions from the pan with a slotted spoon and drain on absorbent kitchen paper. Leave to cool and become crisp before using as a garnish, sprinkled over cooked foods. Can be stored for up to 2–3 days in a covered jar.

RAITA
(CUCUMBER WITH YOGURT)

Serves 4

½ small cucumber

300 ml (½ pint) natural yogurt

15 ml (1 tbsp) chopped fresh mint

salt and freshly ground pepper

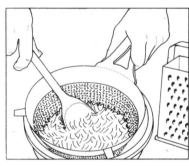

1 Coarsely grate the cucumber. Put in a sieve and squeeze out as much of the water as possible.

2 Put the yogurt in a bowl and stir in the cucumber, mint and pepper to taste.

3 Cover and chill for about 1 hour. Sprinkle the raita with salt before serving.

--- VARIATIONS ---

Substitute fruit for the cucumber such as 1 sliced banana or 1 finely cubed dessert apple. If liked, add 1 seeded and very finely chopped green chilli. Substitute 15 ml (1 tbsp) chopped fresh coriander for the mint.

ALOO KA RAITA
(SPICED POTATO RAITA)

Serves 4–6

450 g (1 lb) potatoes, scrubbed but not peeled

5 ml (1 tsp) cumin seeds

5 ml (1 tsp) coriander seeds

2.5 ml (½ tsp) garam masala (page 140)

1 cm (½ inch) piece of fresh root ginger, peeled and roughly chopped

1 garlic clove, skinned and crushed

1 small onion, skinned and roughly chopped

30 ml (2 tbsp) ghee or vegetable oil

2.5 ml (½ tsp) chilli powder

5 ml (1 tsp) salt

300 ml (½ pint) natural yogurt

paprika, to garnish

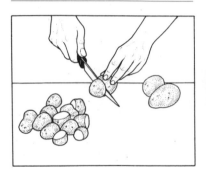

1 Cut the potatoes into 2.5 cm (1 inch) pieces and cook in boiling salted water for about 10 minutes until almost tender. Drain well and set aside.

2 Put the cumin seeds, coriander, garam masala, ginger, garlic and onion into a blender or food processor with 30 ml (2 tbsp) water and work until smooth.

3 Heat the ghee in a frying pan, add the spice paste and cook for 1–2 minutes, stirring all the time. Add the potatoes and fry gently, tossing them to coat in the spice mixture. Stir in the chilli and salt.

4 Remove from the heat and stir into the yogurt. Allow to cool for 15 minutes, then cover and refrigerate for at least 1 hour before serving. Dust with paprika, to serve.

BAIGAN DAHI KA BARTA
(AUBERGINE WITH YOGURT)

Serves 6

1 medium aubergine, about 350 g (12 oz)
300 ml (½ pint) natural yogurt
1 fresh green chilli, seeded and finely chopped
5 ml (1 tsp) cumin seeds, dry fried (page 141)
1 small onion, skinned and finely chopped
salt and freshly ground pepper
30 ml (2 tbsp) chopped fresh mint
mint sprigs, to garnish

1 Place the aubergine in the bottom of a grill pan and grill under a preheated medium heat, turning frequently, for 20–30 minutes. The skin should blacken and char, and the flesh should be very soft.

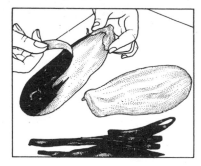

2 Remove the aubergine from the grill and leave until cool enough to handle. Peel off the skin, then chop the flesh.

3 Stir the aubergine into the yogurt with the chilli, cumin, onion, salt and pepper and mint.

4 Cover and chill for about 1 hour. Garnish with sprigs of mint. (This dish will keep for up to 2 days in the refrigerator.)

DAHI ME MILI HUI SABZI
(MIXED VEGETABLES WITH YOGURT)

Serves 4

4 tomatoes, skinned and chopped
1 large onion, skinned and finely chopped
225 g (8 oz) potatoes, boiled and cubed
300 ml (½ pint) natural yogurt
1 green chilli, seeded and very finely chopped
15 ml (1 tbsp) chopped fresh coriander
salt and freshly ground pepper

1 Put the tomatoes, onion and potatoes in a bowl. Mix together gently but thoroughly.

2 In another bowl, stir the yogurt, chilli, coriander and salt and pepper together.

3 Spoon the flavoured yogurt over the vegetables. Cover and chill for 1 hour before serving.

SALAT
(INDIAN SALAD)

Serves 4

225 g (8 oz) carrots, peeled
1 small onion, skinned
½ cucumber
1 green chilli, seeded
1 small green pepper, seeded
2 tomatoes
30 ml (2 tbsp) finely chopped fresh coriander leaves
juice of 1 lemon
salt and freshly ground pepper

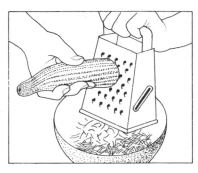

1 Coarsely grate the carrots, onion and cucumber into a salad bowl.

2 Finely chop the chilli, green pepper and tomatoes. Add to the bowl and toss together. Sprinkle with the coriander leaves, lemon juice and salt and pepper to taste and toss again.

3 Cover and chill the salad for 1–2 hours before serving to allow flavours to mingle.

─── VARIATION ───

Add a few roughly chopped unsalted peanuts or cashew nuts.

Yogurt, Cheese and Drinks

Natural yogurt, with its cooling properties, appears at most Indian meal tables in one form or another. Easy to prepare and more delicious home-made, either serve yogurt alone, as a raita (page 152) or refreshing drink, lassi (page 155). A bowl of paneer (soft cheese) can also be included on the menu. This cheese makes a good savoury filling ingredient and is often added to sweet dishes.

Other drinks to accompany Indian food can be fruit juices or cordials. Spiced tea makes an excellent hot alternative.

YOGURT

DAHI
(HOME-MADE YOGURT)

Makes 600 ml (1 pint)

568 ml (1 pint) pasteurised or UHT milk

15 ml (1 tbsp) natural yogurt

15 ml (1 tbsp) skimmed milk powder (optional)

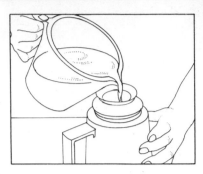

1 Sterilise all your containers and utensils with boiling water or a recommended sterilising solution. Warm a wide-necked vacuum flask.

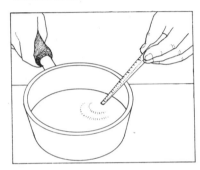

2 Pour the milk into a saucepan and bring to the boil. Remove from the heat and leave the milk to cool to 43°C (110°F) on a thermometer or blood temperature. If using UHT milk it does not have to be boiled; just heated to the correct temperature.

3 Spoon the yogurt into a bowl and stir in a little of the cooled milk. Add the skimmed milk powder, if used, to make a smooth paste. (This helps to make a thick yogurt.)

4 Stir in the remaining milk and pour the mixture into the warmed vacuum flask. Replace the lid and leave for 6–8 hours, undisturbed, until set. Do not move the flask or the yogurt will not set.

5 As soon as the yogurt has set, transfer to the refrigerator to chill. When cold, use as required. Yogurt can be stored for up to 4–5 days in the refrigerator.

CHEESE

PANEER
(HOME-MADE SOFT CHEESE)

Makes about 350 g (12 oz)

2.3 litres (4 pints) pasteurised Channel Islands' milk (Gold Top)

90 ml (6 tbsp) lemon juice

1 Pour the milk into a saucepan and bring to the boil. Remove the pan from the heat and stir in the lemon juice.

2 Return to the heat and boil for 1 minute until the curds and whey separate. Leave to cool for about 1 hour.

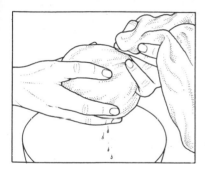

3 Place a piece of muslin over a sieve. Strain the mixture through the muslin and squeeze all the liquid out of the curd. Paneer can be stored for up to 2–3 days in the refrigerator.

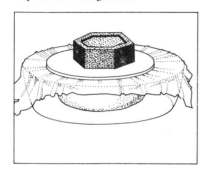

PRESSED PANEER
Tie up the muslin, cover with cling film then press the curds under heavy weights overnight in the refrigerator.

DRINKS

LASSI
(YOGURT DRINK)

Serves 4–6

300 ml ($\frac{1}{2}$ pint) natural yogurt

3.75 ml ($\frac{3}{4}$ tsp) salt

freshly ground pepper

3.75 ml ($\frac{3}{4}$ tsp) dry fried ground cumin seeds or finely chopped fresh mint, to flavour (optional)

crushed ice, to serve

1 Put the yogurt in a blender or food processor. Add 900 ml ($1\frac{1}{2}$ pints) cold water, the salt and pepper to taste and mix for 1–2 minutes. If liked, flavour with the cumin or mint.

2 Put some crushed ice in glasses, pour over the lassi and serve immediately.

MEETHI LASSI
(SWEET YOGURT DRINK)

Serves 4–6

300 ml ($\frac{1}{2}$ pint) natural yogurt

10–15 ml (2–3 tsp) sugar

few drops of rose water, a few finely ground green cardamom seeds, ground cinnamon or honey, to flavour

crushed ice, to serve

1 Put the yogurt in a blender or food processor. Add 900 ml ($1\frac{1}{2}$ pints) cold water and the sugar and mix for 1–2 minutes. Add the chosen flavouring.

2 Put some crushed ice in glasses, pour over the lassi and serve immediately.

MASALEDAR INDIAN CHAI
(SPICED INDIAN TEA)

Serves 4

4 green cardamoms

2 cloves

10–15 ml (2–3 tsp) Indian tea or 2 tea bags, such as Darjeeling

milk and sugar (optional), to taste

1 Put the spices in a saucepan, pour in 600 ml (1 pint) water and bring to the boil. Reduce the heat, add the tea and simmer for about 5 minutes.

2 Pour milk into 4 tea cups and add sugar to taste, if liked. Return the tea to the boil, then strain into the cups. Serve the tea at once.

AAM KA RUS
(MANGO JUICE)

Serves 4

1 large semi-ripe mango

15–30 ml (1–2 tbsp) lime juice

15 ml (1 tbsp) caster sugar

pinch of salt

crushed ice, to serve

slices of lime, to decorate

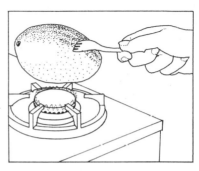

1 Squeeze the mango all over to soften. Spear on to a fork and hold over a flame until the skin is scorched, turning frequently. Leave to cool slightly, then peel off the skin.

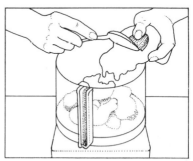

2 Scrape the cooked mango pulp into a blender or food processor and discard the stone. Add the lime juice, sugar and salt, and blend well.

3 Pour the pulp into 4 glasses. Dilute to taste with chilled water and add crushed ice and lime slices to decorate.

NEEBU KA SHARBAT
(FRESH LIME JUICE)

Serves 2

juice of 2 limes

30 ml (2 tbsp) caster sugar

crushed ice, to serve

slices of lime, to decorate

1 Put the lime juice in a jug and add 600 ml (1 pint) cold water and the sugar. Stir until the sugar has dissolved.

2 Put the crushed ice into 4 glasses and pour in the lime juice. Decorate with lime to serve.

GULABJAL SHEERA
(ROSE WATER CORDIAL)

Makes about 600 ml (1 pint)

450 g (1 lb) granulated sugar

juice of ½ lemon, strained

45 ml (3 tbsp) triple distilled rose water

red food colouring

1 Put the sugar in a saucepan and add 300 ml (½ pint) cold water. Stir well and bring slowly to the boil. Boil for 1 minute.

2 Remove from the heat and stir in the lemon juice, rose water and enough red food colouring to give the syrup a dark jewel-like colouring. Cool for 5 minutes then pour into clean dry bottles. Seal.

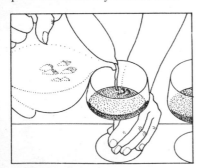

3 To serve, dilute to taste with iced water or soda water. This cordial can be stored in the refrigerator for 10 days.

ADRAK KA SHEERA
(GINGER CORDIAL)

Makes about 4.5 litres (8 pints)

25 g (1 oz) piece of root ginger, bruised

225–350 g (8–12 oz) granulated sugar

5 ml (1 tsp) tartaric acid

½ lemon, sliced

2.3 litres (4 pints) boiling water

1 Place the ginger, sugar (use the larger amount if you like sweet ginger cordial), tartaric acid and lemon in a large bowl. Cover with the boiling water. Stir until the sugar has dissolved, then leave for 3–4 days.

2 Strain the cordial through a muslin-lined filter. Pour into bottles and seal. Leave to mature for 2 days before drinking. Store in the refrigerator for up to 10 days.

SANTARE KA SHEERA
(ORANGE CORDIAL)

Makes about 600 ml (1 pint)

300 ml (½ pint) fresh orange juice

about 450 g (1 lb) granulated sugar

1 Put the orange juice in a measuring jug and pour in enough sugar to raise the level to 600 ml (1 pint). Stir briskly to dissolve the sugar a little.

2 Pour into a saucepan and bring slowly to the boil. Once boiling, remove the pan from the heat and allow to cool for 5 minutes. Pour the syrup into clean, dry bottles and seal.

3 To serve, dilute the syrup to taste with iced water or soda water. Store in the refrigerator for up to 1 week.

GARAM DALCHINI KI CHAY
(HOT CINNAMON TEA)

Serves 6

3 whole cloves

1 cm (½ inch) cinnamon stick

15 ml (3 tsp) Indian tea, such as Darjeeling

50 g (2 oz) sugar

65 ml (2½ fl oz) orange juice

juice of 1 lemon

cinnamon sticks, to serve

1 Put the cloves, cinnamon stick and 1.1 litres (2 pints) water in a saucepan and bring to the boil.

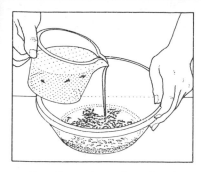

2 Put the tea into a large bowl. Pour over the spiced water and leave to infuse for 5 minutes.

3 Stir, add the sugar, stir again until dissolved and add the strained fruit juices.

4 If necessary, reheat before serving, by placing over a low heat—do not simmer or boil.

5 Strain the spiced tea and serve with the cinnamon sticks.

GHAR KA BANA HUA NEEBU SHARBAT
(HOME-MADE STILL LEMONADE)

Makes about 1.1 litres (2 pints)

3 lemons
175 g (6 oz) sugar
900 ml (1½ pints) boiling water

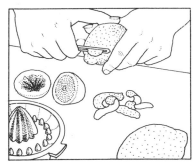

1 Wash the lemons and peel off the rind thinly with a potato peeler. Squeeze the lemon juice and reserve.

2 Put the rind and sugar into a bowl or large jug and pour on the boiling water.

3 Cover and leave to cool, stirring occasionally. Add the lemon juice and strain the lemonade. Serve chilled.

NEEBU JAU KA PANI
(LEMON BARLEY WATER)

Makes about 450 ml (¾ pint)

50 g (2 oz) pearl barley
50 g (2 oz) sugar
juice of 2 lemons

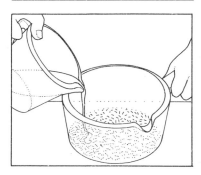

1 Put the barley into a saucepan, just cover with cold water and bring to the boil. Strain off the water and rinse the barley under cold running water.

2 Return the barley to the saucepan, add 600 ml (1 pint) water. Bring to the boil, cover and simmer for 1 hour. Strain the liquid into a jug or bowl, add the sugar and cool.

3 When cold, add the strained lemon juice. It will keep indefinitely in the refrigerator.

NARANGEE SHARBAT
(HOME-MADE STILL ORANGEADE)

Makes about 900 ml (1½ pints)

2 oranges
1 lemon
50 g (2 oz) sugar
600 ml (1 pint) boiling water

1 Wash the fruit and thinly pare off the coloured parts of the rinds, free of all white pith.

2 Put the rinds and sugar into a bowl and pour the boiling water over. Cool, stirring occasionally.

3 Squeeze the juices from the oranges and lemon. Strain the juice and add to the bowl. Mix.

PAAN

And finally, a word about paan. When the feasting is over, the last item an Indian consumes is paan, a digestive and mouth freshener.

Paan is a leaf which is wrapped around a variety of fillings. There are two kinds of leaf; heart shaped, small and sweet Benaresi type or the crisp and slightly bitter Desi leaf. Paan usually contains lime paste, which stains the mouth red, and betel nuts. The filling is secured by a whole clove. Other ideas for fillings are cloves, cardamoms, fennel seeds and perfumed nuts.

Unfortunately, paan is difficult to obtain. So as an alternative, the paan fillings can be offered by themselves. Fennel seeds, with their mildly liquorice taste, are popular especially dry fried (page 141). Green cardamom pods or seeds are better for eating than the whiter variety. Whole cloves can be offered, removing the centre ball first. Betel nut pieces have a mild flavour. In some Indian shops, they are mixed with other seeds, nuts and spices, called suparis, which are sometimes scented. To serve, place the selected items in small attractive bowls set on a tray.

In wealthy Indian homes, paan are stored in special silver or brass boxes called paandaans. These boxes contain compartments for the leaves and different fillings.

GLOSSARY OF INDIAN WORDS AND TERMS

This should provide a useful guide to restaurant menus and terms in cookery books. You should bear in mind that the Indian spelling can sometimes differ.

A

achar	pickle
aam	mango
adrak	ginger
aloo	potato
amchur	dried green mango
amrud	guava
anda	egg
arbi	yam
atta	wholemeal flour

B

badam	almond
bagoong	shrimp paste
baigan	aubergine
bandgobi	cabbage
besan	gram or chick pea flour
bhaji	dry vegetable curry
bharta	lightly mashed vegetables
bhindi	okra or ladies' fingers
bhoona	dry fried or well fried
brinjal	aubergine

C

channa	yellow split chick peas
chapati	unleavened wholemeal bread
chaval/chawal	rice
chhole	spiced chick peas cooked in tomato sauce

D

dahi	yogurt
dal	pulses
dar cheeni	cinnamon
dhania	coriander
dosa	spicy pancakes
dudh	milk
dum/dam	technique of steaming

G

gajar	carrot
ghee	clarified butter
gobi	cabbage
gosht	meat
guda	marrow
guchian	dried Kashmiri mushrooms

gulab	rose water
gurd	jaggary, a kind of unrefined cane sugar

H

haldi	turmeric
halva	very sweet snack
hare	green
hare kayle	green bananas
harimirch	green chillies

I

idli	dumpling
imli	tamarind
ilayachi	cardamom

J

jau	barley
jeera	cumin

K

kadoo	pumpkin
kamal	lotus
karela	bitter gourd
kayle	banana
keema	minced meat
kesar	saffron
khajoor	dates
khas khas	poppy seeds
khatta	sour
kheera	cucumber
khumbi	mushroom
kochikai	red chillies
kofta	meat or vegetable ball
korma	food cooked in yogurt and spices
kutchi	uncooked

L

lasan	garlic
laung	cloves

M

maans	meat
machi/machli	fish
maida	plain flour
makai ka atta	cornflour
malai	cream
masala	a spice mixture
masalewale	cooked dry with herbs and spices
masur	red lentils

matar	peas
meethi	sweet
methi	fenugreek
mithai	Indian milky sweets
mirch	chilli
mooli	white radish

N

namal	lotus seeds
nan	flat leavened white bread
nariyal	coconut
neebu	limes

P

papeeta	papaya
paratha	shallow-fried unleavened wholemeal bread
peelay	yellow
phal	fruit
phoolgobi	cauliflower
piaz	onion
puri	deep-fried unleavened wholemeal bread

R

raita	yogurt with vegetables
rajma	red kidney beans
roti	bread

S

sabzi	dry vegetable curry
sag	spinach
sarso	mustard seeds
seviyan	vermicelli
sharbat	cooling drink
sheera	concentrated drink or syrup
suji	semolina

T

tandoor	a clay oven
taza	fresh
til or gingelly	sesame

V

vark/varak/warak	edible silver leaf garnish
vindaloo/vindalu	sour curry from Goa

INDEX